The Fragrance of Faith

The Enlightened Heart of Islam

The Fragrance of Faith

The Enlightened Heart of Islam

Jamal Rahman

THE BOOK FOUNDATION
BATH, ENGLAND

THE BOOK FOUNDATION
www.thebook.org

Publication Design by Threshold Productions.
Cover Design by Kabir Helminski.

First Book Foundation edition published 2004.

British Library Cataloguing in Publication Data
A catalogue record of this book is available from The British Library

Library of Congress Cataloging-in-Publication Data
The fragrance of faith / by Jamal Rahman.
Bath, England: The Book Foundation, 2004.

ISBN 1-904510-08-6
Includes bibliographical references.
1. Islam. 2. Sufism
I. Jamal Rahman II. The Book Foundation

بسم الله الرحمن الرحيم

Dedication

Dedicated to the memory of my beloved parents, Ataur and Suraiya Rahman.

O my Sustainer, Bestow Your grace upon them,
even as they cherished and nurtured me when I was but a child.

[*Sūrah Al-Isrā*ʾ 17:22-24]

Acknowledgments

All gratitude is to Allāh, Infinitely Compassionate and Merciful.

I am deeply indebted to:

- All my teachers for the generosity of their gifts and blessings.
- My beloved family, especially Kamal and Aysu, for their unconditional love.
- Barbara Trites for her consummate skills and lavishness of spirit in nursing this project from beginning to end.
- Karen Lindquist, Bill Bennett, and Katayoon Naficy for their steadfast and loving support.
- Rabbi Ted Falcon, Rev. Rodney Romney, and Father William Treacy for the sweetness of friendship and the beauty of shared commitment.
- Wayne Teasdale, Melissa West, and Denise Linn for their precious encouragement.
- Kabir and Camille Helminski for their vision and graciousness.
- Hamida Battla for her kind support of intellectual work of this kind.
- Subhana Ansari for her kind and professional editorial assistance.
- And finally, to members of our growing Interfaith Community in Seattle whose genuine love, heartfelt challenges, and shared ideals have made me a better Muslim.

TABLE OF CONTENTS

FIVE PILLARS OF ISLAM

Introduction

MY PARENTS have been my most precious teachers. They taught with love and caring the basics of the Islamic faith and conveyed the spirit of the tradition through example and by a special teaching.

This special teaching I refer to is a learning attained by contemplation on stories and verses. This simple method of teaching and learning is found in many traditions. The profoundest truth is sometimes best expressed by a teaching story or sacred verse that illuminates. Islamic mystics make prolific use of this technique.

Instinctively, a teacher knows which particular story or verse is needed for the student's inner work. Through this process of meditation on the verse or story, subtle shifts can occur within one's being. As one acts on this heart-felt understanding, i.e., begins to live it, one inevitably develops into a higher station.

Once the blush of the Beloved
descends on you,
there is no going back
to being a green apple.
(Traditional saying)

My father acquired his fondness for this technique from his father, Maulana Hedayatullah, a rural spiritual teacher and healer of Northern Bengal. Grandfather made an art form of this technique. He made extensive use of stories and verses in public sermons, healing sessions, and in conversations with intimates and students.

I never met my grandfather, but he is a formidable presence in my life. Most of father's insights on Islām were attributed to my grandfather. Every few months grandfather "appeared" to him. Father never ceased to be astonished, refreshed, and deeply touched by this phenomenon. Everyone in our family felt a special affection and respect for grandfather.

Grandfather spent close to twenty years in intensive study and meditation in Northern India, in the conservative Islamic Deoband School, and later, with free-spirited teachers in other parts of India. Besides theology and mysticism, he also received extensive training in healing techniques. Upon return to his village home in Bengal as a scholar and healer, he was promptly offered the chair of Arabic and Persian studies in prestigious colleges in Calcutta, but he turned them down. He felt called to live and serve in villages.

The community in grandfather's village of Mahdipur built three rooms adjacent to his house to serve as an official school and a place for grandfather to offer guidance and healing to individuals. Grandfather conducted classes for a committed circle of students, usually under the shade of mango trees.

Grandmother was known in the village communities for her ability to heal through her compassionate gaze and tender touch. Even though publicly she stayed in the background because of social conservatism, in private she worked tirelessly in counseling, healing, and empowering scores of women who flocked to her. She was a source of immense support to grandfather; they worked remarkably well as a team.

The word "spaciousness" was very dear to grandfather and this word became an integral part of my parent's vocabulary and mind set.

"Without spaciousness of mind and heart it is difficult to comprehend the Qurʾān," insisted grandfather. "The Holy Book is difficult to grasp. How could it be otherwise?" Grandfather pointed out that in the Qurʾān, the Infinite is seeking expression through the limitations of language. It is as if the entire musical scale is being expressed through one note.

Commenting on the Qurʾān, a *ḥadīth* (a saying of the Prophet Muḥammad ﷺ) is that "its roots lie in the heart of man and its branches or subtle meanings reach high into the sky of mystical knowledge." None understands except "those who possess the inner heart" [*Sūrah Āl ʿImrān* 3:7].

As a teenager, I delighted in the insight of the thirteenth-century Islamic saint, Jalālu'ddin Rūmī, that the Qurʾān is like a shy bride and rather than approach her directly, it is advisable to first bond with her friends, those who possess the inner heart. These are the sages who abound in Islām.

From an early age, I was fascinated by the universally-loved Rūmī. When his heart opened up and his being "burst through the seven worlds," words of pearl-like wisdom and beauty flowed out of him. His scribes wrote them down over a period of years and compiled his utterances into books.

By the grace of God, some of my formative years were spent in countries where Rūmī is studied with awe and devotion: Iran and Turkey. This international traveling was possible because my father was a diplomat. Father was expected to live his life as a teacher and healer in the tradition of his ancestors, but he broke the pattern. He opted to serve in a different capacity. He joined the diplomatic service and went on to become Ambassador of Pakistan and later, after the country separated into two nation states, Ambassador of Bangladesh.

I was apprenticed to friends of my parents who explained to me that Rūmī had penetrated the mysteries of the Qurʾān. I was fascinated by these pious "teachers" who carried with them wherever they went a copy of the Qurʾān and the Mathnawī,[1] a book of sacred poetry by Rūmī. At night they deposited with great care the Qurʾān on the highest shelf of the house and gently placed the Mathnawī under their pillow. The tenderness of my teachers' hearts and the sweetness of their devotion struck a deep chord in my heart.

I was taught verses of the Qurʾān and then invited to chant and

[1] The Mathnawī is a vast six-volume work of exquisite spiritual knowledge in the form of rhyming couplets written in Persian. Rūmī wrote only the first eighteen lines; the rest were dictated over a period of twelve years to his favorite scribe, Ḥusāmuddīn Chelebi.

meditate on selected poetry of Rūmī. Like millions of people, I felt unbounded adoration and veneration for Rūmī's insights which essentially are commentaries on the inner meanings of the Qur'ān.

From my mother I acquired a love of "Mullah Naṣruddīn" stories. The Mullah is a mythological and folklore character who is timeless and placeless, much like the Native American trickster, the coyote, in storytelling. Teachers regularly use Mullah stories to impart teachings.

The Mullah is a village idiot and sage rolled into one. It is said that because he does not aspire to be a teacher, he is truly a teacher. The Mullah is not unlike us, but he is also not like us.

Mother took great joy in planting Mullah stories that have "many levels of meaning" in our subconscious minds. When unexpected insights arose, mother delighted in what she called "blossoms and fruits."

My father and mother were remarkable teachers, deeply versed in Islām and possessed of the precious spaciousness that grandfather referred to repeatedly. They rooted their children in the teachings of Islām but encouraged us to nourish those roots by learning about other traditions. Growing up in Muslim, Hindu, Buddhist, and Christian countries, we visited mosques, temples, synagogues, and churches. My parents genuinely believed that a sincere appreciation of other faiths deepens and widens one's own inner faith. An appreciation of other traditions is not about conversion; it is about completion. Many times, especially in India, I heard Mahatma Gandhi's beautiful words often in our household: "It is a sacred duty of every individual to have an appreciative understanding of other religions."

When friends of father applauded him for being a modern Muslim, he replied that appreciation of other traditions is in the true spirit of Islām. The Qur'ān mentions that many prophets and religions came before the Prophet Muḥammad ﷺ; "do not make any distinctions between them" [*Sūrah An-Nisā'* 4:152]. When delegations of non-Muslims visited the Prophet Muḥammad, he invited them to conduct their services in the mosque for "it is a place consecrated to God."

The same friends were surprised to hear from mother that the

Prophet Muḥammad ﷺ was a revolutionary when it came to advocating women's rights. Mother had much to say on this matter. In seventh-century Arabia, a strictly patriarchal society, the Prophet insisted that women receive property, inheritance, and divorce rights—something unthinkable for that period. Mother readily brought up the issue of the Prophet's marriages. For twenty-five years the Prophet was married to his beloved wife, Khadījah ؓ. Take note, said mother, that Khadījah was fifteen years the Prophet's senior and as a successful business lady, the Prophet's employer. "Is this not radical for any age?" asked mother. After Khadījah's death, the Prophet lived ten more years and in that time married several wives. Two of his wives were Jews and one Christian; all of his wives, save for one, were slaves, widows, or divorcees, considered discards in that community. The Prophet directed attention to the great need to break down social and cultural prejudices.

Mother minced no words in explaining that some so-called "Islamic" practices had their roots not in the Qurʾān but in male-dominated cultures. The veiling of women was a case in point. Another was the issue of a man marrying four wives in special circumstances. The Holy Book emphasizes that this is permissible only if the multiple marriage is just, fair, and most important of all, if the husband is able to divide his affection equally between his wives.[2] In *Sūrah An-Nisāʾ*, the Qurʾān clearly states that "you will never be able to deal equitably with all your wives, however much you want" [4:129]. If some men choose to avoid and flout this verse, it is to suit the convenience of the male ego.

Ultimately, it is the ego that needs to be worked on. Transformation of the ego is our life purpose. It is the untamed ego that tries to "possess" a religion or prophets. Spirituality cannot be roped or caged; prophets belong to no one and everyone. Every religion is humankind's heritage.

My parents frequently employed the metaphor of every religion being a flower in God's garden. Mother enchanted her guests by singing a poem by Tagore in Bengali:

---

[2] A woman does have the right to specify monogamy in her marriage contract, as did the granddaughter of the Prophet, Amīnah.

I came to offer You a flower
But You must have all my garden
It is Yours.[3]

Three Principles and Five Pillars of Islām

Rūmī said of his lifelong study of the Qur'ān, "I have taken the marrow from the Qur'ān and thrown the bones to the dogs." This was not meant to be disrespectful but to underline an essential point: it is paramount to absorb the essence of a tradition and live it and not be distracted by hair-splitting disputes.

Muslims traditionally receive guidance and inspiration from four sources: first, the Qur'ān; second, the collected sayings of the Prophet ﷺ and examples of his life (called *ḥadīth* and *sunnah,* respectively, and classed as one); third, resources in the community, e.g., the wisdom of elders and scholars; and fourth, individual reasoning.

I have chosen verses of the Qur'ān and *ḥadīth* to highlight the three principles and five pillars of Islām. I have then elaborated on them, drawing on the wisdom of Rūmī's prose and poetry, teaching stories, and, finally, teachings of my family exemplified by grandfather.

The three principles of Islām are surrender, faith, and moral virtue. The five pillars are the profession of faith, prayers, almsgiving, fasting, and pilgrimage.

Arrangement of this Book

Spiritual teachers know the specific needs of their students. Not long before my parents passed away I asked them what were the most important teachings from the Qur'ān for me to focus on in my journey. They offered the following:

- Always be grateful.
- Do the real work.

---

[3] Rabindranath Tagore, *Fireflies* (New York: Macmillan Publishing Company, 1955), p. 142.

- ❖ Do this work with compassion and mercy for yourself.
- ❖ Remember that at your core, you are infused with the breath of God.
- ❖ Be flexible.
- ❖ Meditate on your death.

I start the book with four pieces of prescriptive wisdom from my parents followed by insights about the three principles and five pillars. I end with two more wisdom pieces chosen by my parents.

The stories, verses, and practices in this book are those that I personally have spent time with and cherish. My ardent wish in writing this book is to share something of the fragrance of Islām that my beloved parents spread wherever they went.

Please note that God, who is beyond gender, is variously invoked in this book as He, She, and It.

Throughout this book there are notations of numbers in brackets. These refer to chapter (*sūrah*) and verse (*āyah*) of the Qurʾān. The first time the Prophet Muḥammad ﷺ is mentioned in a paragraph, his mention is followed by the symbol for "May the peace and blessings of Allāh be upon him." The symbol عليه السلام follows the first mention of other prophets in a paragraph, "Peace be upon him." When Muḥammad's companions are mentioned, they are followed with the symbol for "may Allāh be pleased with him" or "may Allāh be pleased with her."

WISDOM FROM PARENTS

1

Gratitude

Whatever is in the heavens and on earth
extols the limitless glory of God
[*Sūrah Al-Jumu*ʿ*ah* 62:1]

ONE MORNING, the Mullah discovered, to his dismay, that his donkey had disappeared. His helper, companion, and source of livelihood had vanished! Frantically, he began to search. His neighbors joined in, looking in the hills and valleys, far and wide, but to no avail. The donkey was missing. At dusk, the neighbors turned back to give Mullah the sad news. They found him in the Town Square on his knees, hands stretched out, praising Allāh and exclaiming, "Thank you, Allāh! Thank you, Allāh!" Puzzled, the townsfolk asked the Mullah if he knew that his donkey was lost, maybe forever. "I know, I know," beamed the Mullah. "But I have so much to be thankful for. Imagine what could have happened to me if I was on the donkey!"

The Mullah has tapped into a great secret of the Qurʾān: gratitude. In giving thanks, we are participating in life's greatest mystery, the relationship of creation to Creator. The Qurʾān says there is nothing that does not proclaim the Creator's praise. When our inner faculties are awakened, we hear melodies of constant praise in the swaying of branches, the rustle of leaves, and in the dignified stillness of earth and stones. The *ḥadīth* mentions that a bird, after sipping water, tilts its head heavenward not only for the water to flow through but for praise and thanks to flow heavenward!

In expressing gratitude, we humans take our place in the wheel of life. Our souls continuously and instinctively praise our Creator. Gratitude brings this expression of the soul into space and time.

When we are not grateful, we cover or hide God's blessings from us, and we fail to enjoy the link with the Creator that every moment provides. (Incidentally, the original meaning of "infidel" in Islām came from the Arabic *kufr*: one who is "hidden" from God's blessings because of ingratitude.) When ungrateful, we are not able to experience enjoyment. To take things for granted is one of the greatest failings of human life.

Mullah Naṣruddīn announced a reward to anyone who found his lost donkey. The reward was his donkey! "Are you crazy?" the townsfolk asked the Mullah. "Not at all. You do not understand that the joy of recovering what was lost is greater than the joy of possessing it!"

Grandfather cultivated gratitude at every step. On Fridays, after noon prayers, he retired to his room for a half hour ritual. Eyes closed, hands on heart, grandfather melted into a trance. Softly, at times in silence, he intoned continuous words of heart-felt thanks to God. Interspersed with these words were recitations of Qurʾanic verses. At times his body swayed with his outpourings; other times he was still. Tears poured profusely down his cheeks soaking his shirt. Curious family members who secretly peeked in invariably burst into tears.

Knowing the power of gratitude, grandfather asked that we strive to be grateful even in times of affliction. When we hold gratitude in our hearts in difficult times, we are giving thanks for unknown blessings already on their way. Grandfather believed that besides compassion and awareness, gratitude is the other key available to us for unlocking the mysteries of the Universe.

Reflections

It is beyond me to express Thy praise.
Thine own praise of Thyself alone can express what Thou art.[4]
(*Ḥadīth* of the Prophet Muḥammad ﷺ)

For sixty years I have been forgetful, every minute,
but not for a second has this flowing toward me stopped or slowed.[5]
(Rūmī)

Practices

- Make gratitude an integral part of your life. For example, before eating, make it a habit to send heartfelt thanks to grains, plants, fruits, and animals who sacrifice themselves for your nourishment. Upon arising and before sleep, make it a habit to say a prayer of thanks to your Creator. You can never overdo your expression of thanks to God.
- When you receive a gift, thank the giver and remember to hold gratitude for the Giver. If someone gave you a beautiful and expensive hat, wouldn't you be grateful to that person? But shouldn't you be even more grateful to the One who gave you the head on which to put the hat?[6]

---

[4] Constance E. Padwick, *Muslim Devotions* (Oxford, England: One World Publication, 1996), p. 91.
[5] Jalālu'ddin Rūmī, Mathnawī I:2084, in *Open Secret*, translated by John Moyne and Coleman Barks (Putney, VT: Threshold Books, 1984), p. 74.
[6] A similar description of this insight appears in several traditions.

2

The Real Work

On the earth are signs for those of inner certainty,
and also in your own selves. Will you not then see?
[*Sūrah Adh-Dhāriyāt* 51:20-21]

UNDER A WELL-LIT streetlight, the beloved eighth-century saint Rābiᶜa was engrossed in looking for a lost key. Soon her neighbors joined in the search, but without success. "Where did you drop it?" they asked, hoping to focus on that area. "Oh, I did not lose my key here but over there in my house," replied Rābiᶜa. Surprised and bemused, they respectfully asked why she did not look for the lost key in the house. "That is because my house is dimly lit, but out here it is so much brighter under the streetlight," she explained.

The neighbors could not help laughing; they shook their heads in disbelief. This was Rābiᶜa's opportunity to impart a teaching. She addressed them: "Friends, it is clear that you're intelligent. Then why is it that when you lose your peace of mind or happiness, perhaps because of a failed relationship or job, you look for what was lost out there and not in here?" Rābiᶜa pointed to her chest. "Did you lose your joy out there or in here? Do you avoid looking inside you because the light is dimmer, and therefore, more inconvenient?" This insight struck a deep chord in her neighbors.

This story of Rābiᶜa had supreme significance for my parents and grandparents. Spend time with the story, for it has exceptional powers, they insisted.

The Qurʾān remarks that "In time We shall make them fully understand Our messages in the utmost horizons and within themselves" [*Sūrah Fuṣṣilat* 41:53]. Repeatedly the Holy Book asks, "Will you not see?" Several times the Qurʾān states that unless there is a change in our "inner selves," there will be no change in outer conditions or in the flow of blessings from God [*Sūrah Al-Anfāl* 8:53, *Sūrah Ar-Raʿd* 13:11). Reality is both outer (*ẓāhir*) and inner (*bāṭin*) [*Sūrah Al-Ḥadīd* 57:3].

To do our inner work is highly inconvenient, but to know who we are is our primary task. We need to confront who we really are. This work leads to unfolding from within, and it is necessary to usher in the fullness of our being. A common refrain of grandfather to his students was this reminder: to do the work is to become the work.

The Rābiʿa story, grandfather explained, is also about the inner meaning of *qiblah.* The word literally means "in the direction of" and relates to Islamic prayers. Five times a day Muslims prostrate in prayer in the direction of the Kaʿbah[7] in Mecca. In prayer, the *qiblah* becomes the sacred direction.

In dealing with our issues and searching for solutions for life, may we focus our gaze and attention in the right direction. This sacred turning will happen when we apply ourselves to do what my parents called the "real work," i.e., work on ourselves.

Reflections

You know the value of every article of merchandise
but if you do not know the value of your own soul,
it's all foolishness.[8]

(Rūmī)

---

[7] This large cubic stone structure draped in black cloth stands in the center of the Grand Mosque in Mecca. In the Eastern corner of the cube is a black stone which legend says was brought down to earth by the Angel Gabriel. According to tradition, the foundation was laid by Adam ﵇ and the building constructed by Abraham ﵇ and Ishmael ﵇. The Kaʿbah establishes the direction of prayer for all Muslims around the world.

[8] Jalālu'ddin Rūmī, Mathnawī III:2652, in *Jewels of Remembrance*, versions by Camille and Kabir Helminski (Putney, VT: Threshold Books, 1996), p. 26.

The thing we tell of can never be found by seeking,
yet only seekers find it.[9]
(Bāyazīd Bisṭāmī)

[9] Llewellyn Vaughan-Lee, editor, *Travelling the Path of Love* (Inverness, CA: The Golden Sufi Center, 1995), p. 27.

3

Compassion

In the name of Allāh, Infinitely Compassionate, Infinitely Merciful
[*Sūrah Al-Fātiḥah* 1:1]

A *ḤADĪTH* says: "All that is in the revealed books is contained in the Qur'ān; all that is in the Qur'ān is contained in the opening *sūrah* (chapter) called *Fātiḥah*; all that is in the *Fātiḥah* is contained in the *Basmala*." The formula by which God is invoked to bestow His benediction is the *Basmala*: "*Bismillāh-ir-Raḥmān-ir-Raḥim.*" The words mean "In the name of Allāh, Infinitely Compassionate and Infinitely Merciful." These words open every chapter of the Qur'ān save for one. God's Compassion and Mercy are cited one hundred and ninety-two times in the Holy Book. Compassion and Mercy are the essence of God.

There is a deeper message in the *Basmala*, explained grandfather. He went to great lengths to explain the inner meaning of this verse: Allāh wants us to be compassionate with ourselves.

In doing this work of transformation, of giving birth to our real Self, grandfather repeatedly reminded everyone to be compassionate with themselves. "Can we learn to receive our pain with tenderness and love? Have mercy, for we are precious in God's eyes. Little do we know who we are, where we come from, and where we are going. Our beings deserve to be touched by compassion every step of the way." Grandfather was emphatic on this point, "Whatever work you do on yourself, if you do not do it with compassion for yourself, you will not make much progress."

Compassion was a mantra grandfather invoked unabashedly. While explaining a practice for inner development, he stopped in mid-sentence and asked his students two questions, one followed quickly by the other. "Do this practice with what?" "With compassion," the students would reply in chorus. "Compassion for whom? "For myself, for myself," the students joined in smiling and laughing.

To be compassionate with self does not mean that you avoid or deny what needs to be looked at and worked on in aspects of your personality. You do whatever is necessary, but with the energy of compassion and mercy. Grandfather explained what compassion meant to him. "Observe your personality with the eyes of the soul; work on what is necessary in your personality but with the qualities of your soul. The primary qualities of the soul are mercy, gentleness, and graciousness. The soul makes no judgment and is filled with unconditional love."

Grandfather highlighted a simple point, "If I cannot be compassionate with myself, I cannot truly be compassionate with others. I might learn the mechanics of being kind and think I am merciful and loving, but that compassion is incomplete."

Keep in Heart, Always

True compassion encompasses everyone, including the offender. Does this mean that the offender and the offense are excused and not dealt with? Not at all. You do what is necessary, but with qualities of the soul. Grandfather used a favorite insight, taught by his teachers, to explain: "Do what is right, but please do not shut the person out of your heart." Follow this principle and you have tapped into the beauty and power of compassion.

When you are locked in a just combat with a wrongdoer, remember you are fighting the antagonism, not the antagonist. Do what is necessary, but do not banish the antagonist from your heart. For example, an honest judge presides over the trial of an offender. He does what is right: he sentences the man to life imprisonment. He can proclaim this sentence with contempt and disdain for this man, eager in his heart to banish this "scum of the earth" offender into oblivion. This is one energy. The judge can mete out the same sentence but with another energy, by not keeping the offender's soul out of his heart. He reads the sentence with solemnity and respect. He makes sure that the offender is accorded his due dignities; he ensures he is not maltreated in prison. Maybe the judge even prays for the offender, sending light from his heart to the soul of the convicted person. So the same sentencing can be carried out with two different energies. One is from the ego; the other is from the soul. Compassion is energy from the soul that has the power to shift heaven and earth.

God as Compassion

Some say that God is so tenderhearted and overflowing with grace that if God could die for us, God would. This is impossible, so we have to die for God. This is the mystery of our journey. But know that God's exquisite and Infinite Compassion sustains us on every step of our path.

A *ḥadīth* says: "Whoever approaches Me walking, I will come to him running, and he who meets Me with sins equivalent to the whole world, I will greet him with forgiveness equal to it."

The great saint Bāyazīd Bisṭāmī heard God's voice in a dream: "O Bāyazīd, I shall expose your spiritual infidelity to your followers, and they will stone you." Bāyazīd shot back, "O Beloved, if you do so, I shall expose Your tender heart and compassion, how forgiving You are when someone repents, the truth that your Mercy is infinitely greater than your Justice, and so no one who knows this will ever obey Your laws again." God became silent and relented.

If God is truly compassionate, why then does God not reveal Itself to us? Is it not cruel of God to hide His Face, causing doubt and dismay in this world? Wise teachers explain that the veils between us and God are necessary. If God's Beauty and unspeakable Majesty were to flare out in wave after wave of blinding lightning without veils, no one could endure them. Rūmī says that when God reveals Its veiled Self to a mountain, the mountain laughs and is covered with grass, flowering trees, and rose bushes. These inebriate the birds and the mountain becomes a garden of birdsong. If God revealed Itself without veils, the mountains would dissolve into ashes and dust. So the veils between us and God enable God in

Her tenderness and compassion to sustain and nourish us as we are.

Our basic nature is noble and deeply compassionate. If we do not know this, it is because we are unaware. We have not reached a state of wakefulness and so we sometimes act from states of fear rather than from knowing within us. Rūmī says that he who begrudges water to the thirsty is unaware of the mighty river flowing next to him.

As we soften the armor and defenses that we have built around the heart, we become aware of a divinely lit lamp in us. It is this flame of compassion and love in the heart that dissolves shadows within and without and illuminates the world.

Reflections

How should Spring bring forth a garden on hard stone?
Become earth, that you may grow flowers of many colors.
For you have been heart-breaking rock.
Once, for the sake of experiment, be earth! [10]
(Rūmī)

Practices

- Grandfather rejoiced in a practice in which he asked his students to add a word of endearment to their names and to make a lifelong habit of using that affectionate term with their names whenever talking to themselves. The truth is that we talk to ourselves very often and a lot of the talk is negative. Become aware of this internal conversation. Make it a practice to relate to yourself with affection and compassion.
- Grandfather called himself *Heda bhai* (*bhai* in Bengali means brother) and conversed with brother Heda quite often, with compassion, of course. This practice Grandfather claimed encourages one's divine identity to step forward.

---

[10] Jalālu'ddin Rūmī, Mathnawī I:1911-1912, in *Rūmī Daylight*, versions by Camille and Kabir Helminski (Boston, MA: Shambhala Publications, 1999), p. 51.

4
Inner Majesty

It is He who has made you His representatives on earth
[*Sūrah Al-Anʿām* 6:165]

A SCHOLAR approached the Mullah and said, "I hear you know techniques that can give me revelations beyond what books and scriptures can impart."

"Indeed it is so," replied the Mullah, "but only on condition that you follow to the letter what I instruct."

"Agreed!"

The first week's assignment was to kneel in the marketplace three times daily, kiss the ground, grab his ears, and sing a particular song. The Mullah reassured the skeptical scholar that this would bring amazing revelations. A week later the scholar returned to report his progress. He was furious! Everyone in the market had roared with laughter and derision.

"I felt like a fool! A total, complete fool! An absolute fool!"

The Mullah exclaimed, "Wow! Fantastic! Marvelous! For just one week's work, this is a profound revelation, wouldn't you say?"

Indeed we are fools! We are far more than our personality; inside us resides resplendent Majesty, a sun more radiant than any sun we can imagine. But we have little idea of this.

The Qurʾān points out that God molded Adam[11] عليه السلام and Eve from water and clay and out of Infinite Graciousness infused them with His Divine breath. All the angels save for one prostrated to the Divine Spirit

[11] Mentioned twenty-five times in the Qurʾān, Adam عليه السلام is referred to twenty-one times as a collective noun, the "human"—a symbol for humanity.

in Adam and Eve. The Qur'ān says that the human being is *fiṭrah* (originally good and noble). Also, the human being is called *insān,* which has its roots in *uns*, meaning intimacy.

In the Islamic tradition, Adam عليه السلام and Eve were banished to earth after committing transgressions in the garden of paradise. Adam and Eve begged for forgiveness. God out of Infinite Compassion readily forgave them and, furthermore, honored them. "We have fashioned you in the best of forms," explains the Qur'ān [*Sūrah At-Tīn* 95:4] and even though humans are capable of "the lowest sin and folly" [*Sūrah At-Tīn* 95:5], Allāh has appointed Adam and Eve and their descendants to the exalted position of being viceroys of Allāh on earth.

The Holy Book tells humankind "We offered the Trust to the heavens, the earth and the mountains. They refused it and were afraid, yet man accepted it" [*Sūrah Al-Aḥzāb* 33:72]. The human being is blessed with Divine Spirit, is a bearer of the Trust, and a representative of God on earth.

You surpass this world and the next in value.
What am I to do if you do not know your own worth?
Do not sell yourself short, for you are extremely precious.[12]
(Rūmī)

Why do we not easily know our worth? How is it that we are so unaware of the incredible potential within us? Rūmī gives us some insights.

He states that, first of all, we tend to define ourselves outside of ourselves. We name ourselves by our outward appearances, such as our profession, bank account, etc. We miss the inward reality.

Secondly, we received our soul without much work or toil. How should a man or woman who inherits know the value of wealth?

O so-and-so, you don't know the value of your own soul
because from His abundance, God gave it to you freely.[13]

[12] Jalālu'ddin Rūmī, *Signs of the Unseen*, translated by William Thackston (Putney, VT: Threshold Books, 1994), pp. 16-17.

(Rūmī)

Thirdly, awakening to who we really are is the purpose of life and the bewildering mystery of our journey: foredoomed to slumber so we might awaken; foredoomed to forget so we might remember.

Sooner or later we shall know our real self. How could it be otherwise? Inside, explains Rūmī, we breathe the fragrance of the Friend.[14]

Reflections

You are a ruby in the midst of granite—
how long will you try to deceive us?
We can see the truth in your eyes –
so come, return
to the root of the root of your own self![15]
(Rūmī)

Practices

❖ When you encounter a difficult person, deal with the personality and do what is right. Protect yourself. But please be aware that he or she is more than personality. Can you restrain judgments, knowing that when you react in judgment, you risk criticizing the person's essence? You begin to judge the Grand Artist who made the person.

---

[13] Jalālu'ddin Rūmī, Mathnawī VI:4209, in *Jewels of Remembrance*, versions by C. and K. Helminski, p. 187.
[14] Jalālu'ddin Rūmī, *Love is a Stranger*, versions by Kabir Helminski (Putney, VT: Threshold Books, 1993), p. 80.
[15] Dīwān-i Shams-i Tabrīzī 120, in *The Sufi Path of Love*, translated by William Chittick (Albany, NY: State University of NY Press, 1983), p. 339.

Three Principles of Islam

FIRST PRINCIPLE: SURRENDER

5

The Journey of *Islām*

The only religion in the sight of God
is self-surrender to Him
[*Sūrah Āl ʿImrān* 3:19]

THE JOURNEY of surrender is at the heart of Islām; the word *Islām* means to "surrender in peace." The Qurʾān declares that the only true religion in the sight of God is self-surrender to Him. Muslims believe that to be a slave of Allāh is to be freed from slavery to the ego.

Surrender is the lifelong practice of listening to and acting on the needs of the soul, allowing the Divine and not the ego to be the center of Reality. Surrender becomes the soul's dynamic role in the Will of God, giving up limited will to participate in Cosmic Will. This giving up is not a resignation, but a deep honoring of one's real self.

When you have set in the west,
then your light will rise from the east.[16]
(Rūmī)

Grandfather was particularly eager to emphasize one central point: We cannot accomplish surrender by just saying, "O God, I surrender to You." We must have something to surrender. Surrender requires a pre-

[16] Chittick, *The Sufi Path of Love*, p. 193.

requisite.

Rūmī says, "Free will is the attempt to thank God for His beneficence." We have work to do on ourselves, without which surrender is meaningless. This is the work of awareness, integration, and "seeking refuge in God." "O sifter of the dust," says Rūmī, "your intellect is in fragments, like bits of gold scattered over many matters. You must scrape them together, so the royal stamp can be pressed into you."[17]

"It is important to understand," grandfather explained, "that the work is not about destroying the ego. The ego cannot be eliminated, but it can be transmuted by expanding into a greater Light, a higher Will, a higher Intelligence."

The Prophet Muḥammad ﷺ encapsulated the work involved in the journey of surrender in two of his celebrated sayings: "He who knows himself will know his Lord" and "Die before you die," i.e., die to your ego before dying a physical death. Clearly, the work requires a lifetime of self-vigilance and spiritual practices.

First Step

The first step in the journey of surrender starts with a longing that boils up from within, an inner calling to go beyond the ego. In a *ḥadīth qudsī*,[18] Allāh says: "Between Me and you there are no veils, but between you and Me there are seventy thousand veils." In each of us lies an innate longing to travel beyond the ego and remove the veils between self and the Creator. It is the Allāh within us yearning for Allāh. When we acknowledge and embrace this mysterious and abiding ache, we become a seeker.

---

[17] Jalālu'ddin Rūmī, Mathnawi IV:3287, in *The Essential Rūmī,* translated by Coleman Barks with John Moyne (New York, NY: HarperCollins, 1995), p. 241.

[18] The *ḥadīth* are divided into two groups: *qudsī* (sacred) and *sharīf* (noble). In the former, God Himself is speaking. The latter are the Prophet's utterances and acts.

6

Longing of the Soul

I was a secret treasure and I longed to be known . . .

LIKE MILLIONS of Muslims, grandparents rhapsodized over an exquisite *ḥadīth qudsī* in which Allāh says:

I was a secret Treasure
and I longed to be known
and so I created the worlds.

The truth about this longing is that it is cosmically encoded in us. Essentially, it is a longing of the soul—a sigh from the heart of the seeker to the heart of the Beloved. It is a longing that drives the wanderer ever onward.

It is wise not to avoid, suppress, or bemoan this longing. There is sacredness to this ache. Honor the feeling and be present with it. Gently encompass it with your compassion and understanding. Follow the scent of its musk. It has the power to lead us out of our lives of quiet desperation and make seekers out of us. As we become travelers, magically, the Way appears.

In their lifetime, grandparents worked with hundreds of people who today would be diagnosed as suffering from clinical depression. Grandparents respected their sadness as having roots in something deeper.

Two things they did worked remarkably well. Grandparents received their pain with mercy, gentleness, and love. In silent empathy, they spent time with them, often holding hands and stroking their hair. Second, they helped create for them authentic community—a circle of family members and friends who volunteered to be in regular touch with the depressed person. Members of the circle were responsible for nudging, persuading, and accompanying the depressed member into going for walks, doing breathing and physical exercises, and participating in spiritual practices.

Many of these depressed friends moved through their sadness. Some became spiritual adepts and a significant number volunteered to help others.

Majesty of Longing

Grandfather told stories of Ibrāhīm ben Adḥam to illustrate the beauty and power of this longing.

The mighty prince of eighth-century Balkh, Ibrāhīm ben Adḥam, possessed everything a person might want, but still felt an emptiness inside, an aching for something he knew not what. Relentlessly, he pursued his desires: feasting, gambling, womanizing, and hunting. Once while chasing a stag, he was separated from his retinue. In the heat of the hunt, the stag, a magical being, suddenly turned his head towards the prince and spoke, "O Ibrāhīm ben Adḥam, were you born for this?" and vanished! The words seared into the prince's soul and stirred up deep questions in him.

Another time, as the prince gazed into a stately mirror, he saw himself walking towards a long, dark tomb, further and deeper, until finally in the presence of what he perceived was a just judge, again, the question was asked, "Were you born for this?" Something shifted deep inside of him.

In a third incident, the prince half-asleep, reclining on his couch, entertained the idea that maybe it was time in his life to explore spiritual matters. The prince fell asleep. Suddenly a series of loud thuds on the palace rooftop woke him up. Startled and confused he shouted, "Who's up there? What's going on?"

"Oh, it's nothing," replied a voice from the rooftop. "Go back to sleep. I'm just looking for my lost camel."

"That's absurd," replied the prince, "How can you be searching for your camel on top of the roof?"

"O heedless one," came the reply, "it's no more absurd than you, dressed in silken pajamas, lying on a gold-sewn couch, searching for Truth."

Ibrāhīm ben Adhạm was awakened. He was transformed. The prince gave up his kingdom and became a beggar, a servant of service begging for alms of mercy from God.

The story of the prince epitomizes a person who follows the fragrance of his longing musk and, in a visionary moment, gives up his external kingdom for inner majesty.

The journey of surrender starts with a longing, an abiding sigh from the soul that puts us on the path and gives us the strength to endure difficulties. It's the same longing that prompts the salmon to use every ounce of its strength to swim upstream against a mighty river, intent on the spawning pools high in the mountains; a longing that leads birds to embark on the hazardous journey of their migration, thousands of miles away to their unknown destination. Sooner or later, this pull from within puts us on the Path. In the end, we tire of everything except the soul's journey back to God.

sultan, saint, pickpocket;
love has everyone by the ear
dragging us to God by secret ways

I never knew
that, God, too, desires us.[19]
(Rūmī)

[19] Vaughan-Lee, *Travelling the Path of Love*, p. 145.

Reflections

Listen to the reed and the tale it tells,
how it sings of separation:
Ever since they cut me from the reed bed,
my wail has caused men and women to weep.[20]
(Rūmī)

The source of my grief and loneliness is deep in my breast.
This is a disease no doctor can cure.
Only union with the Friend can cure it.[21]
(Rābiᶜa)

---

[20] Jalālu'ddin Rūmī, *The Rūmī Collection,* selected and edited by Kabir Helminski (Boston, MA: Shambhala Publications, 1999), p. 145.
[21] Vaughan-Lee, *Travelling the Path of Love*, p. 48.

7
Two Veils

Health and Wealth

THE MULLAH, as ferry captain, was privileged to have on board some learned and wealthy dignitaries—scholars, lawyers, and business people. To pass the time they engaged the Mullah in conversation and egged him to talk about his favorite topics. They amused themselves watching the Mullah become animated as he talked of God, invisible realms, and the need to polish the heart so that one is in a "fitting state to come into the presence of the Beloved." Some in the group chuckled softly. These were people of science with little use for speculations and superstitions.

Presently, a storm arose. It grew worse. The boat began to toss and turn helplessly. All was lost, it appeared. Amazingly, many among the people of reason got on their knees imploring and pleading with God to save their lives. Promise after promise was offered—the kind of promises people make when desperate. The Mullah, calm and poised, walked between them and advised, "Friends! Friends! Now, now! Steady! Don't be reckless with your goods."

Turning to the lawyers, he said, "Come on, drive a harder bargain"; to the business people, "Hey! What about the bottom line?"; to the scholars, "Now, really, first do more research before making promises." To all of them he declared, "Avoid entanglements as you have in your life so far." Suddenly, the Mullah, peering in the distance shouted, "Ahoy! Ahoy! I see land!" The story goes that the passengers got off their knees, celebrated, and indeed avoided further entanglements.

Alas, says Rūmī, there are two veils that may muffle our longing and obscure our sight of the path to self-realization: health and wealth.[22] All other veils are offshoots of these two. Unless we are truly awake, these veils get in the way of our becoming seekers.

When our health is robust and rosy, we feel unshakable; when secure in wealth, power, or circumstances, we feel indestructible. This may lull us into superficialities and stagnation. Any talk of invisible realms appears distant, irrelevant, even irritating at this time. But should the veil be torn apart because suddenly health suffers calamities or one's security dissolves, something awakens in us and we yearn for deeper meaning. We begin to seek help from a Higher Source. "Please help me," we plead, "I can't do this by myself."

May we awaken to deeper realizations in our life! May we become aware of our longing, greet the ache with understanding and compassion, and allow it to make true human beings out of us! Praise! Praise to all early-waking grievers, exclaims the Andalusian poet, ^{c}Adī b. ar-Riqā^{c}:

I was sleeping, and being comforted
by a cool breeze, when suddenly a gray dove
from a thicket sang and sobbed with longing,
and reminded me of my own passion.

I had been away from my own soul for so long,
so late-sleeping, but that dove's crying
woke me and made me cry. Praise
to all early-waking grievers![23]

---

[22] *Fihi ma Fihi* 233/240, Chittick, *The Sufi Path of Love,* pp. 238-239.
[23] A blessing in the Introduction to Book IV of the Mathnawī, Barks and Moyne, *The Essential Rūmī,* p. xvii.

8

The Ego

He who knows himself will know his Lord
(*Ḥadīth* of the Prophet Muḥammad ﷺ)

THE QURʾĀN tells us that there are three stages of *nafs* in the human. *Nafs* is loosely translated as the little self, ego, the "water and clay" part of us. Mainly through the work of self-vigilance supported by spiritual practices, the *nafs* is transformed and surrenders to God.

The three stages of *nafs* are as follows: a self that inclines towards wrongdoing; a self that is able to discern and make choices; and a self that is at peace.

Self-vigilance enables one to understand the nature of the ego and the trance states it holds us in. This vigilance combined with practices such as prayers and fasting dissolves the trance and allows one to submit to God and grasp "the most trustworthy handhold" [*Sūrah Luqmān* 31:22]. One is then at peace, knowing that "truly God's guidance is the only guidance" [*Sūrah Al-Anʿām* 6:71].

The practice of self-vigilance is called *murāqabah*, a word derived from the Divine name *Ar-Raqīb*, the Aware, the Watchful. This practice involves three elements: being present to one's self, witnessing one's self continuously, and exercising compassion for one's self.

Grandfather underlined the three elements of *murāqabah* in his own unique way. To underscore the first element of being present, grandfather reminded his students of the saying: "A Muslim is a son or daughter of the present moment." He explained the second element, witnessing, by borrowing a Vedic metaphor from his Hindu friends: "We are like two birds sitting on the branch of a tree. One bird pecks away at the fruit of life. The fruit could be sweet or bitter. The other bird simply witnesses without judgment. Remember both birds are us, the participant and the witness." Grandfather emphasized the third element, compassion, by saying that the first two elements are like pillars and the two pillars stand on the ground of compassion. "If the ground is shaky, the pillars will fall," grandfather remarked. This was his way of underlining the need at all times for compassion towards self.

Work with the ego involves considerable exertion. In Islām, this exertion is called *jihād*.[24] Surely this *jihād* is holy, seekers claim, because if God wanted He could have put perfect beings on earth. Instead He sent ordinary humans like us. To make exertions to know ourselves is a holy, mysterious task ordained by God.

The true human being, spiritual teachers like to say, makes exertion over his or her self; the superficial human being over other people's egos. One must not be fooled into thinking that transmuting the ego is an easy task. Constantly, one has to be watchful and firm. The ego does not give up its center stage position easily.

By contemplating on simple stories, one begins to understand the nature of one's ego, its trance states, and the importance of self-vigilance. Self-awareness unclasps the ego's hold on us.

In the tradition of their forebears, my parents delighted in telling us special stories about the ego, for us to contemplate on.

---

[24] Islamic scholars make a distinction between the lesser and greater *jihād* on the basis of an often-repeated saying of the Prophet after the critical battle of Badr: "You have returned from the lesser *jihād* to the greater *jihād*." To the exhausted warriors, the Prophet explained, "The greater *jihād* is the struggle with what is in your breast. Your worst enemy is between your two sides." In the lesser *jihād*, sanction is given to defend oneself against oppressors and to protect "those who have been unjustly driven from their abodes merely because they said, 'Our Lord is Allah'" [*Sūrah Al-Ḥajj* 22:39-40]. The Qur'ān emphasizes: "but do not commit aggression for, truly, God does not love aggressors" [*Sūrah Al-Baqarah* 2:190].

Reflections

May a wind from His Garden breathe you this secret:
It is not only I who am speaking here
But you, too, your own soul, your own heart –
Only for you are we ever apart.[25]
(Rūmī)

Practices

❖ Observe yourself with kindness. With a vigilant but gentle eye, witness yourself at all times. Keep a journal. Note down what you discover about yourself. Shine the light of awareness on all parts of your personality. This practice of compassionate awareness and gentle witnessing is like a sun whose light dissolves shadows and gives life to what needs to blossom and flower in your being.

[25] Andrew Harvey, *Light Upon Light* (Berkeley, CA: North Atlantic Books, 1996), p. 183.

9

The Nature of Ego

Thank God I came along . . .

ONE MOONLIT NIGHT the Mullah, on one of his walks, peered into a well and was horrified to find that the moon had fallen into the bottom of the well! Eager to be of service to the world, he rushed home to get a rope. After tying a hook at one end, he flung the rope into the well. "Worry not, sister Moon," cooed the Mullah encouragingly, "Succor is at hand." The hook got hold of something. With all his might, the Mullah heaved and puffed, and as the hook loosened something, he fell on his back. He was now able to see the moon restored to its proper domain. He felt elated. "Thank God I came along," said the Mullah to himself. "Imagine the consequences if I did not happen to pass by this particular well."

Reflections

❖ The ego has a highly exaggerated opinion of itself.

10

Patterns

The cheese sandwich

IF THERE is one story that my grandparents and parents relished telling and hearing again and again, it has to be the story of the cheese sandwich.[26]

During lunch break at work, the Mullah was getting exasperated. Every time he opened his lunchbox, it was a cheese sandwich. Day after day, week after week, it was the same—a cheese sandwich.

"I am getting sick and tired of this lousy cheese sandwich," complained the Mullah repeatedly. His co-workers gave him some advice; "Mullah, you don't have to suffer through a cheese sandwich over and over again. Tell your wife to make you something different. Be firm with her if you have to."

"But I'm not married," replied the Mullah. By now, puzzled and confused, his colleagues asked, "Then who makes your sandwiches?" "Well, I do!" replied the Mullah.

Practices

❖ With compassionate mindfulness become aware of the cheese sandwich patterns in your life in which you might be stuck.

[26] The Mullah's lunch has varied depending on country and century.

11

Excuses

Who are you going to believe, me or the donkey?

A NEIGHBOR knocked on the Mullah's door, asking to borrow his donkey. The Mullah was reluctant and so made up an excuse. "I'd like to, but someone else has already borrowed the animal." As luck would have it, just at that time the donkey began to bray. "But I hear the donkey!" exclaimed the neighbor. The Mullah, seeming indignant and offended, raised his voice, "Now, who are you going to believe, me or the donkey? I am glad this came to pass. I could not, in any case, ever lend my donkey to someone with your mental disposition!"

Looking at our excuses, we might be surprised at the length and breadth to which we go to cover half-truths. With painstaking complexity and creativity, we construct an intricate scaffolding of excuses to support our misalignments. This tendency to blame circumstances and other people creates lopsidedness in our personalities.

Some of our excuses are exotic. Mullah sneaked over a wall into a rich neighbor's garden and began to fill his sack with a variety of vegetables. The owner chanced to see the Mullah and ran over shouting, "What are you doing here?"

"I was blown over here by a high wind."

"And how come the vegetables are uprooted?"

"Well, Allāh be praised, I was able to grab hold of them to prevent myself from being swept away."

"Then why are the vegetables in your sack?"

"Indeed, life is a mystery. That's exactly what I was contemplating on before you so rudely interrupted me."

Some of our excuses are falsely pious.

The Mullah was feasting himself on a huge roasted chicken. A beggar peering through the window implored the Mullah to share some of the chicken with him. "Gladly and willingly," came the reply, "for I believe in sharing, but this chicken unfortunately belongs to my wife. My hands are tied. I am eating only because my wife has asked me to."

In the next story, the Mullah is candid about his excuse. A neighbor dropped by to borrow the Mullah's clothesline.

"Sorry, it's in use at this time. We are drying wheat flour by putting it on the clothesline."

"Drying flour on the clothesline! That must be a difficult task."

"Far less difficult than you think if you don't want to lend the clothesline!"

Practices

❖ List your excuses and look at them gently. Notice how some excuses are filled with energy and creativity. They're impressive! Know that a person with this much energy and creativity also has the capacity and potential to become enlightened. Only the direction needs changing.

12

Fear

What will happen tomorrow?

A WHITE COW lives on a green island and all day long eats the grass. During the night, the cow becomes thin as a blade with anxiety, "Oh my! What shall I eat tomorrow? I'm doomed." Tomorrow comes; the grass has grown. The cow chomps and munches the grass in the day. Night comes, and again the cow shakes with fear. "What will happen tomorrow?"

The story of the cow, says Rūmī,[27] is the story of our lives. Because we do not go beyond the frontiers of the ego and have little understanding of the power and grace of the Invisible, we live in a trance of fear.

Rūmī continues: "You came from nowhere, from a sperm in the womb. Did you have any idea what roads you would take before you took them? Yet you have definitely arrived. In exactly the same way and with exactly the same mercy and mystery and strange providence, you will be brought to thousands of other worlds."[28]

When sensations of fear vibrate in us and we avoid and deny them, they grow. Darkness feeds them and in the shadows they assume frightening shapes that can overwhelm us. Only in the light of awareness will the fear-distortions melt.

Perhaps everything that frightens us is, in its deepest essence, something that needs our attention and love. Looking at our fears little by little and with compassion dissolves the trance.

---

[27] Jalālu'ddin Rūmī, Mathnawi V:2855-2869, *Say I Am You,* translated by John Moyne and Coleman Barks (Athens, GA: Maypop, 1994), p. 78.

[28] (Paraphrased) Thackston, *Signs of the Unseen,* p. 124.

Reflections

Don't burden your heart with thoughts
of livelihood; livelihood will not fail.
Be constant in attendance at the Divine Court.[29]
(Rūmī)

[29] Mathnawī II:454, C. and K. Helminski, *Rūmī Daylight*, p. 103.

13
Attachments

It's not the uphill or the downhill—
it is the load.

A SAINT who knew the language of animals asked a camel whether he preferred going uphill or downhill. The camel said, "What is important to me is not the uphill or the downhill—it is the load!"[30]

In the ups and downs of life, it's the burden of attachments to what the Qurʾān calls the "tinsel of life" that exhausts us. The proverbial bag we carry gets heavier and heavier and holding on to it is draining. We suffer.

The Qurʾān laments that humans attempt to deny their mortality through incessant acquisitions. The Holy Book asks that we make exertions to understand the nature of desire in the *nafs* (ego).

Grandfather told a story of the desire bowl of the ego; it was one of his favorites. A mighty emperor felt pity for an old beggar limping with a begging bowl outside his palace. The guards summoned the beggar inside.

"Old man, name your desires. I feel moved to fulfill them," commanded the emperor.

"Only that Majesty upon High can do that. You cannot even fill my bowl," replied the beggar, in reality a self-realized Master with a magical bowl.

Challenged, the emperor ordered rubies and emeralds to be put into

[30] A Chishti story found in Idries Shah, *The Way of the Sufi* (London, England: Penguin Books, 1974), p. 134.

his bowl. Astonishingly, they vanished! Whatever riches were heaped into the bowl, they simply disappeared. The bowl swallowed them up. In desperation, the emperor asked, "What bowl is this?"

"This is the desire bowl of the ego, your Majesty, always desiring but never satisfied. This bowl swallows whatever is put into it. Understand this and you become an emperor; otherwise, you become a beggar."

Catching Monkeys

In the village of Mahdipur elders explain the consequences of clinging to our desires by describing a traditional way of catching monkeys.

In a hollow coconut, a small hole is carved through which food is put in, and the coconut is tied to a tree. The smell of the food attracts the monkey who, by straightening its fingers, manages to squeeze its hand in the hole. It clutches the food but is unable to bring out the enlarged fist. The hunters arrive; the monkey shrieks, jumps up and down, but not once does it think of letting go of the food. The monkey is caught! How comical and strange, we might think. But how quick are we to let go of our attachments? Because we do not, how many peculiar situations do we find ourselves in?

Aversion and Craving

Know that aversion and craving are both attachments, two sides of the same coin. In a teaching story, Moses عليه السلام, on his way to talk to God, met a holy man who implored him to ask God why, in spite of devoted practices day and night, he received so little results. On his return, Moses delivered the message from God, "It's your beard!"

"But of course," exclaimed the holy man, "How true! For half my time I spend trimming and making beautiful my beard and every two hours I keep looking at my beard in my little pocket mirror. From now on, I am resolved to remove this obstacle." Henceforth, every time a hair or stubble appeared on his face, with fervor, immediacy, and determination, he plucked it out. No longer would the beard be a barrier between him and the Light. Years passed. No enlightenment. Anxiously, the servant of God awaited the reply from his Creator. Moses عليه السلام delivered the answer: "It's your beard!" The practitioner of Truth got it this time! First it was his obsessive love of his beard, and now it was the obsessive harshness with his beard. Both are obstacles. In that instant, the holy person let go and became filled with light.

Reflections

- The Prophet ﷺ was asked, "What is worldliness?" He answered, "Everything that makes you heedless and causes you to forget your Sustainer."

14

Two Basic Laws

Is it not enough that your Sustainer is a witness?
[*Sūrah Fuṣṣilat* 41:53]

MY FATHER shared with me two basic laws; it was essential, he explained, that I take both laws to heart. Accepting the two laws is a litmus test of progress made in knowing one's ego. By embracing the two laws, the ego is no longer a "commanding master" and surrender to God becomes easier.

First Basic Law

The first law states that whoever's approval you seek, you become imprisoned to them. This is a law of the created world.

My father impressed on me that it was truly important to ponder on this insight. When he felt that I had embraced this insight, he provided commentary that had been repeated for centuries: "Simply choose your jailers with care and deliberation." The Qur'ān says, "If one desires the rewards of this world, let him remember that with God are the rewards of both this world and the life to come" [*Sūrah An-Nisā'* 4:134].

Father delighted in telling the story of Tansen. In South Asia, the name of Tansen evokes awe. This master musician, in the court of the mighty Mughal emperor Akbar of the sixteenth century, possessed a voice of unimaginable beauty. When he sang, legend says, angels danced and trees and flowers bowed in sweet respect. Emperor Akbar was determined to meet the master who taught Tansen to sing like this. On the way to the mountain cave where the teacher lived, the emperor heard the master sing. The emperor swooned into unconsciousness. When he came to, he exclaimed, "Tansen! Tansen! Your voice is magical. But what I heard today is the music of the spheres! It is divine! Can you not sing like that? What gives your master's voice that unspeakable uniqueness?" Tansen replied, "Your majesty, it's simple. I sing for you. My master sings for that supreme Majesty, the Emperor of all Emperors. That is what gives his voice that enchanting quality."

The beauty of what we say and do comes from singing to the highest and deepest in us.

Second Basic Law

The second law states that whatever you say or do, some will praise and some will blame. Can you come to terms with this law? My father encouraged me to contemplate deeply on a Qur'anic verse: "Is it not enough that your Sustainer is a witness?" [*Sūrah Fuṣṣilat* 41:53].

The second law is reflected in a well-known Mullah story. Mullah, his grandson, and his donkey ambled through the marketplace on their way home. The Mullah overheard a conversation: "Look, two travelers and a beast of burden, yet they insist on tiring themselves out." Immediately, the Mullah perched himself on the donkey. Down the road, there were more murmurs. "Look! Any wonder why the younger generation turns out disgruntled and disrespectful? That man on the donkey looks old enough to be wise in years but he lets that boy, tender in age, and fragile in body, suffer so." Instantly, the Mullah got off and put his grandson on the beast of burden. Further in the marketplace, more muted conversations: "Look! A perfectly robust boy enthroned on the donkey while his grandfather shuffles painfully under the searing sun! How we spoil our young ones and later ask, "What did we do wrong?" This time, both the Mullah and the grandson embarked on the donkey. More whispers: "No wonder life is harsh. The heavens punish us for the way we abuse Allāh's dumb creatures. Silently that poor donkey suffers under the burden of the young and old." Quickly, grandfather and grandson disembarked, lifted the donkey, balanced him on their shoulders and started walking. Down the road came scornful laughter.

The more you become immersed in the higher Self, the less you are enslaved to what others may think. You relate directly to the world's Beloved and not to the world's opinion.

Reflections

I want to sing like birds sing,
Not worrying who hears or what they think.[31]
(Rūmī)

Practices

- ❖ Ask yourself: "Whose approval do I seek in my life?" Then choose your jailors with care and deliberation.
- ❖ Remind yourself that no matter what you say or do, some will praise and some will blame. Accept the law.

[31] Andrew Harvey, *The Way of Passion* (Berkeley, CA: Frog Ltd, 1994), p. 178.

15

The Divine Exchange

Die before you die
(*Ḥadīth* of the Prophet Muḥammad ﷺ)

IN A TIME-HONORED STORY, God comes down to earth in the guise of a beggar and pleads with two men for coins. One reluctantly gives a measly coin; the other, several coins. The beggar transmutes the coins into gold and returns them to the astonished men. God can only give back to you what you are willing to give Him. What we offer God is primarily the work we have done on ourselves.

To die to the ego is about a divine exchange: we give up attachment to our little self in exchange for the Higher Self. We make a commitment to be attentive to the desire of the Beloved and not the ego. To die to one's ego is not just a struggle on one level but an opening to a higher level.

This commitment to the Beloved was already made by our souls in those eternal realms. The Qur᾿ān talks about *Alast*, the primordial covenant between God and humankind as yet unborn, i.e., before souls descended to earth in the form of humans. God asked, "Am I not your Lord?" Our souls responded, "Yes! Yes! We witness it." [*Sūrah Al-Aʿrāf* 7:172]. Thus we had surrendered our soul to the Beloved before our earthly existence. Our work on earth is to bring this state of surrender into consciousness and to live it.

We reach a stage in our life where the following words of the Qur᾿ān resonate deep inside of us:

Say: 'Behold, my prayer,
and my acts of worship,
and my living and my dying
are for God alone,
the Sustainer of all the worlds."
[*Sūrah Al-Anʿām* 6:162]

What an amazing exchange surrender is! "Who indeed should be so fortunate?" exclaims Rūmī, "An Ocean wooing a drop! In God's name, in God's name, sell and buy at once! Give a drop, and take this Sea full of pearls."[32]

Can you find another market like this?
Where,
with your one rose,
you can buy hundreds of rose gardens? . . .
For one weak breath,
the divine wind?[33]
(Rūmī)

In the process of this divine exchange comes a deep knowing that God is lovingly mindful of our minutest needs and that we are the obstacles in the way. Less and less do we feel the need for control as we relax into the embrace of God and feel a peace that is indescribable.

In a *ḥadīth qudsī,* Allāh says of His adorer in this state of submission: "I become the hearing by which he hears, the sight by which he sees, the hand with which he grasps, and the foot with which he walks."

Reflections

It suits the generous man to give money,
but truly the generosity of the lover

---

[32] Mathnawī IV:2621-2622, K. & C. Helminski, *The Rūmī Collection,* p. 179.
[33] Mathnawī IV:2611, 2613, Barks and Moyne, *The Essential Rūmī,* p. 153.

is to surrender his soul.
If you give bread for God's sake,
you will be given bread in return;
if you give your life for God's sake,
you will be given Life in return.[34]
(Rūmī)

This is how I would die
into the love I have for you:
as pieces of cloud
dissolve in sunlight.[35]
(Rūmī)

Practices

- In clear, practical terms grandfather elaborated on a practice that was an essential part of surrender to be done for a lifetime. Make it a habit in everything you say or do to ask yourself, "Does my speech or action derive from a place of divine attributes within me: truth, love, compassion, beauty? Or do they spring from a place of the little self in me: fear, pettiness, jealousy?" Be mindful of the question and make conscious efforts to originate from your soul. No matter how inconvenient, choose to honor your "soul need." The Light takes care of the obstacles. Have faith.
- Grandfather was quick to point out that if you lapse and succumb to a petty or selfish impulse in you, remember to be merciful with yourself and be utterly hopeful. The Universe lovingly provides a stream of opportunities to help you connect with your soul.

[34] Mathnawī I:2235-2236, K. & C. Helminski, *The Rūmī Collection*, p. 140.
[35] Jalālu'ddin Rūmī, *Birdsong*, versions by Coleman Barks based on translations by A.J. Arberry (Athens, GA: Maypop, 1993), p. 30.

SECOND PRINCIPLE: FAITH

16

Īmān

. . . a light by which you shall walk
[*Sūrah Al-Ḥadīd* 57:28]

THE QUR'ĀN says that God has faith in humanity. The way of man is to be worthy of this enormous trust that God reposed in humanity. We need to grow in faith (called *īmān* in the Holy Book).

When Adam ﷺ was being created by God, the angels were hesitant for "he will spill blood and make mischief in the land." God replied, "I know what you do not know" [*Sūrah Al-Baqarah* 2:30]. Out of Infinite Graciousness, God breathed His spirit into Adam and Eve. As part of a Divine plan, God appointed the human being as *ʿabd* (servant) and *khalīfah* (vice-regent) of God.

In the astonishing mystery of our existence and our journey on earth, our lives are filled with paradoxes, bewilderment, and doubt. The Qur'ān says, "By the token of time, verily humankind is in loss" [*Sūrah Al-ʿAṣr* 103:1-2]. A Muslim needs to build faith in God, His angels, His revelations, His apostles, and the Last Day—the Day of Judgment.

"Trust Allāh," counsels the Qur'ān. It says, "If Allāh is your protector, none can overcome you, but if He forsakes you, then who can help you?" [*Sūrah Āl ʿImrān* 3:160]. Know that the cultivation of faith provides a light by which you shall walk.

Grandfather stressed the importance of being a *mu'min.* One who is obedient to God's laws is a Muslim, but one who has the deep inner certainty of faith is a *mu'min.* This inner certainty of faith, or *īmān,* has to build up from within. The Prophet ﷺ said, "*Īmān* is confession with the tongue, a verification with the heart, and action of the body."

Muslims are advised to pray, recite the Qur'ān regularly, and be in the company of those "who are in awe of God." These practices help one develop faith. In addition to these practices, grandfather emphasized two more facets of faith-building to his students: have your own experience of Truth and develop a relationship with your inner teacher.

In his youth, grandfather had left his village for several years to study at an Islamic divinity school in northern India and later to continue his learning with some well-known spiritual teachers. He was grateful for the learning but realized that his inner certainty came not so much from the school or teachers but really more from his personal experiences along the way.

Grandfather was convinced that the greatest spiritual teacher resided within one's self. It was necessary to seek out teachers who could help one connect with one's inner teacher and grow an inner faith.

Reflections

Faith is the bird that feels the light and sings
While the dawn is still dark.[36]
(Tagore)

[36] Tagore, *Fireflies*, p. 203.

17

Experiences

He who tastes, knows

A FRIEND called on the Mullah, bringing with him a few ducks he had hunted in the wild. Together, they prepared a large pot of delicious duck soup and enjoyed a hearty meal. The next day the Mullah received a visitor, "a friend of the friend who brought you the duck." The Mullah fed him duck soup. The following day another visitor arrived, calling himself, "a friend of the friend of the friend who gave you the ducks." The Mullah graciously gave them duck soup. The subsequent day another caller, "a friend of the friend of the friend of the friend" dropped by. The Mullah seated him and brought him a bowl of hot water. Eagerly, the guest tasted the soup, then exclaimed in disappointment, "What is this? This is no duck soup." "Yes, it is," insisted the host. "This is the soup of the soup of the soup of the duck!"

Most of our rigidly held beliefs are a watered down "soup of the soup" version of Reality. They do not rise up from within us. We borrow from someone else's beliefs and hearsay. We abide in what grandfather called "borrowed certainty."

However sacred or authoritative the writings of holy books, it is one's deepest experience of them that is the ultimate truth. Deepening of faith requires participation of our being; it requires the engagement of our mind and heart. Faith cannot abide in borrowed certainty.

Once you truly experience with your mind and heart, your inclination to invest in theories and concepts diminishes. "He who tastes, knows" is a popular saying.

A theoretician was passing by a river and spotted a dervish sitting by a riverbank, the curve of his neck bared to the sun. Eager to test a theory, the scholar slapped loudly the exposed neck with his palm. The dervish, screaming with pain, turned around to hit him, but the scholar said, "Wait! Before you hit me, please tell me, the sound we heard, was it from the neck hitting the palm or the palm hitting the neck?" "O misguided scholar," replied the dervish, "the pain I feel does not leave me room to theorize and speculate. You would not understand because you feel no pain!"[37]

Through heartfelt experiences one matures; through the richness of experiences faith blossoms and one's being transforms until, as the sages say, one becomes "rosy red with illumination." What is fascinating is that at this stage one begins to radiate beauty and authenticity in everything one says or does.

Students of grandfather often remarked that they learned not only by listening to his words but also by watching the glow in his face as he talked of Allāh; the beautiful movement of his hands as he stressed a point; and the glistening in his eyes as he touched on his favorite themes: compassion for self, awareness, and gratitude to God.

All masters lovingly push us to dance through life experience after life experience. They preach through example. Rūmī, in his deepest moments of anguish, danced and whirled; in times of ecstatic joy, he danced and whirled.

Dance, when you're broken open.
Dance, if you've torn the bandage off.
Dance in the middle of the fighting.
Dance in your blood.
Dance, when you're completely free.[38]
(Rūmī)

---

[37] Mathnawi III:1380-1385, translated by R. Bly, *The Rūmī Collection*, p. 91.
[38] Mathnawī III:95-97, *This Longing*, translated by Coleman Barks and John Moyne (Putney, VT: Threshold Books, 1988), p. 55.

Reflections

- Ibrāhīm ben Adḥam, the eighth-century king who gave up his kingdom to become a seeker of truth, came upon a large stone with the inscription: "Turn me over and read." On the back of the stone, he discovered another inscription: "You do not practice what you know. Why do you seek what you do not know?"

- A disciple thanked his Shaykh for teaching him caution. "These days," said the student, "I think not once or twice but three times before recklessly jumping in." "Once is enough," replied the master.

18

Inner Teacher

Every Muslim is his own priest
(*Ḥadīth* of the Prophet Muḥammad ﷺ)

THE MULLAH was deathly ill, lying on his bed, his life ebbing away, surrounded by family, friends, and his wailing wife. The doctor examined the Mullah at length, turned to the Mullah's wife and spoke with eloquence, "The Qur᾿ān says, 'Only Allāh, the Light of the Heavens and Earth, is immortal.'[39] O honorable wife of the Mullah, the Mullah is no more. He is dead." As the doctor continued, the Mullah was feebly heard to say, "No, wait! I am alive! I am alive!" "Quiet, quiet!" retorted his wife, "The doctor is speaking. Don't argue with the doctor!"

At every opportunity grandfather pointed to our slavish dependence on pundits and authorities. A popular village idiom says: "When you are moved by a bird in song, do you feel the need to ask it for credentials?" Degrees and titles blind us. Sadly, we fail to cultivate and bring out the teacher within us, our inner guide.

The Jesus of your spirit is within you:
ask his aid,
for he is a good helper.[40]
(Rūmī)

---

[39] *Sūrah An-Nūr* 24:35 and *Sūrah Al-Baqarah* 2:255.
[40] Mathnawī II:450, C. and K. Helminski, *Rūmī Daylight*, p. 103.

Outer Teachers

Do we need outer teachers? Of course we do. To connect with our inner teacher it is wise to consult a guide who knows the inner landscape.

Spiritual teachers say that we are like water that needs to cook and boil. The teacher is an intermediary, a kettle, between the fire and us. In another metaphor, we need the radiance of the sun to grow and evolve. It is difficult to stare into the naked sun, but the moon is easy and delightful to gaze upon. The moon is none other than the Sun's overwhelming radiance taking beautiful form. We need moon-like teachers to guide us.

Students living in far-flung villages in northern Bengal sought advice from grandfather about studying with teachers in their local area. Islām has no organized priesthood. The Prophet Muḥammad ﷺ said, "Every Muslim is his own priest." The Qurʾān says that between humanity and God there are no intermediaries.

However, one needs teachers who help the inner teacher in us to emerge. Choosing a teacher wisely is important. Grandfather advised discernment.

Be wary of fire-breathing preachers and teachers who are noisy, aggressive, and competitive; those who raise a lot of dust and din.

As it is, he's all fire and no light,
all husk and no kernel.[41]
(Rūmī)

The Mullah started preaching in the Town Square. At first, a large crowd gathered. The Mullah was loud, emphatic, and dramatic. Slowly, as the days rolled by, the crowd thinned out until not one person showed up. But daily the Mullah continued to preach in his aggressive fashion. Asked why he continued in the empty town square, the Mullah explained, "In the beginning, I had hoped to change these people. If I still shout, it is only to prevent them from changing me!"

Sheer numbers of listeners or followers does not authenticate a

---

[41] Mathnawī VI: 3926, Barks and Moyne, *The Essential Rūmī,* p. 183.

teacher. To prove his point, the Mullah one day went to the speaker's dais in the town square and bellowed out, "O people! O people! Listen to me. Do your want riches without work, knowledge without difficulties, truth without falsehood, attainment without effort, progress without sacrifice?" The Mullah repeated his message several times, and each time the crowd multiplied, swelling in numbers. They began to clamor, "Yes! Yes!" Finally his point proven, Mullah said, "Excellent...thank you! I only wanted to know. You may rely on me to tell you about it in good time!"

Authentic wisdom does not clamor for attention. There is no need to aggressively advertise one's existence. Mawlana Rūmī asks, "Does a magnet cry out to the iron filings, 'O please, come to me'?"

The true teacher is deeply compassionate. He or she sees all beings coming from the same sacred Source, healing, integrating, and transforming their personalities usually with some exertion and suffering, and returning to the Source. He helps us to become not like the teacher, but more our real selves. This, grandfather emphasized, is a key insight.

Hidden Teachers

Grandfather marveled at the phenomena that once the inner teacher awakens in us, we become aware of hidden teachers everywhere and in everything.

The renowned master, Ḥasan of Basra, teased a child who was lighting a candle. "Little one, tell me where did this magical flame come from?" The child instantly blew out the candle and asked, "You tell me, where did the flame go?" This awakened something deep in him. The little child, he said, was a big teacher.

One teacher mastered the art of concentration by watching a cat absorbed in its prey before pouncing. Another learned fearlessness by observing a thirsty dog at the edge of a pond. Eager to drink, but frozen and scared by its reflection, eventually the dog plunged in. The fearful image disappeared and he was able to quench his thirst.

A verse from the Qur'ān says, "And in the earth are signs for those whose faith is certain" [*Sūrah Adh-Dhāriyāt* 51:20]. All around us are signs and messages pointing the way. The mystics with their heightened consciousness are eloquent in their expressions: the song of birds and the voice of insects are all means of conveying truth to the mind. In flowers and grasses are woven messages; in the rustling of leaves there are specific instructions; at dawn the breeze has secrets to tell. The Universe, aware of our minutest needs, is eager to serve us at every step.

We are asked to honor our teachers, but especially the wise teacher in each of us. Adore outer teachers, but know that this comes from adoration of one's inner teacher.

Reflections

The teacher kindles the light
The oil is already in the lamp.
(*Ḥadīth* of the Prophet Muḥammad ﷺ)

Practices

❖ Listen to authorities and experts but intuit whether this is in harmony with your inner teacher. Does it correspond with what your heart tells you? Can you distinguish your inner teacher from the demands of your ego? Become silent, go within, and listen. By reflecting in this way again and again, the wise teacher within begins to emerge. Initially, you might hear several voices in you. If you listen to the voice of the ego and make a mistake, be compassionate with yourself and persist. With practice you learn discernment and eventually connect with the voice of your real guide.

THIRD PRINCIPLE: MORAL VIRTUE

19

Iḥsān

Bring to God a sound heart
[*Sūrah Ash-Shuʿarāʾ* 26:89]

THE QURʾĀN remarks, "Allāh enjoins justice, beautiful conduct, and generosity towards those close to you" [*Sūrah An-Naḥl* 16:90]. We are asked to develop *iḥsān,* a word derived from *ḥasana,* "to be good or beautiful." *Iḥsan* is variously translated as righteousness, beautiful conduct, or moral virtue. In *Sūrah Āl ʿImrān* [3:134, 3:148] and *Sūrah Al-Māʾidah* [5:93] the Qurʾān says "God loves the morally virtuous," the *muḥsin.*

For all that we receive, again and again, from the "infinite bounty of God" [*Sūrah Al-Anfāl* 8:29], what can we offer in return? The Qurʾān advises: "Bring to God a sound heart."

The Queen of Sheba felt indebted to King Solomon عليه السلام. She sent him mule load after mule load of glittering gold. Her envoys were stunned to find that even the streets of King Solomon's kingdom were paved with gold! "All I really wanted," said King Solomon, "is a heart of gold."

In the Qur'an, the Biblical Joseph عليه السلام is a symbol of nobility, knowledge, and beauty. In a story related by Rūmī,[42] one of Joseph's friends, visiting as a guest, ponders what he could possibly bring Joseph as a gift that would be worthy of his perfection. He gives Joseph a mirror and says, "This is all I can offer you, a mirror, so that by gazing into it you may see the perfection of your beauty."

---

[42] Mathnawī I:3150-3227, Barks and Moyne, *The Essential Rūmī,* pp. 139-142.

Purify your being so you reflect in yourself the loveliness of your Creator. As you cleanse yourself, your being is pierced by a sweet, divine light. A light from within rises and a light from the heavens descends, enveloping you with what the Qur'ān describes in a celebrated verse as "Light upon Light" [*Sūrah An-Nūr* 24:35].

Chilla

Adjacent to the mosque in Mahdipur, grandfather constructed two small rooms. The rooms served as space for students and friends to engage in exercises of purification. In a practice called *Chilla* (inspired by the Prophet's habit of spending time in silence in the caves of Mecca), the practitioner cloistered himself in the room for ten to forty days and nights immersed in prayer, meditation, readings, introspection, and silence. The practitioner ate sparingly from a meal provided once a day.

Some evenings grandfather visited to advise about issues that cropped up, to interpret dreams, and to prescribe specific meditations and recitations. At the end of the purification period, in a sacred ceremony marked by silence, grandfather and other students greeted the practitioner by embracing him. Bystanders jostled to be as close as possible in order to catch a glimpse of the indescribable glow coming from the practitioner's face.

Reflections

The flame met the earthen lamp in me
And what a great marvel of light![43]
(Tagore)

The noblest of deeds is simply this:
that the devotee purify himself
of the notion of his own purity.[44]
(Tustarī)

---

[43] Tagore, *Fireflies*, p. 228.
[44] Farid al-Din Attar, *Tadhkirat al-Auliya*, p. 314.

Practices

- The Prophet ﷺ explained how best to practice beautiful conduct: act and speak in this world as though you are seeing God, and if you cannot see God, know that God sees you.

20

Humility

Seek help in patience and prayer;
truly this is hard, except for the humble-minded.
[*Sūrah Al-Baqarah* 2:45]

THE SAINT Bāyazīd Bisṭāmī, deep in meditation, experienced a wondrous vision. He was transported into celestial realms and was ushered into the place where God's Throne sits. All around were angels singing praises of Divinity and circling the seat of God. Utterly awed and overwhelmed, the saint mumbled, "How indescribably fortunate and blessed that God sits here with you!"

A voice emanating from the Throne replied, "How amazing! We are told that God dwells in pure and humble hearts."

Practice humility, say the elders, and you begin to connect with an indwelling Divinity within you. The practice of humility is about dissolving self-centeredness. The person who has traveled beyond self-centeredness realizes he is nothing and yet is not separate from Divinity. One bows lower and lower to the mystery and beauty of this paradox. This bowing brings him or her true dignity.

Have you not noticed, asks the Qur'ān, that all things that God has created "cast their shadows to the right and left, bowing themselves before God in all humility?" [*Sūrah An-Naḥl* 16:48]. "Do not walk proudly on earth" cautions the Holy Book, "you cannot cleave the earth nor can you rival the mountains in stature" [*Sūrah Al-Isrā'* 17:37]. The beloved of God are those who "walk the earth in humility" and when the ignorant address them they say "peace" [*Sūrah Al-Furqān* 25:63]. They are aware that "this is hard except for the humble-minded" [*Sūrah Al-Baqarah* 2:45].

The Qur'ān encourages every Muslim to engage in prayers so that through the postures of bowing and prostrating to God one inculcates the precious quality of humility (*khushū*ᶜ) inside. "Call upon your Lord humbly and secretly," advises the Qur'ān [*Sūrah Al-A*ᶜ*rāf* 7:55].

Spiritual masters make an interesting observation about humility: bowing down is not about appearances but about essence. Humility does not mandate a specific demeanor, posture, tone of voice, or choice of words. Humility is about an internal shift.

A famous Shaykh contemplated on some verses of the Qur'ān and was deeply touched. He raised his hands to the heavens crying out, "O God, truly Yours is the Glory! I am nothing! I am nothing!" His senior disciple, who was with him in the mosque, felt deeply inspired by this act of humility. Together with his Shaykh, they began prostrating and rolling on the floor of the mosque wailing, "O God, I am nothing! I am nothing!"[45]

A beggar who was passing by was affected by this. Very soon he was also on the floor crying out, "I am nothing! I am nothing!" The Shaykh, noticing the beggar, nudged his disciple in the midst of the outpourings and said, "Look! Just look at that! Just see who thinks he is nothing!"

Reflections

Who humbles himself
Like the earth under him.
Receives the cover of mercy
Like the sky over him.
(Traditional saying)

When a seed falls into the ground,
it germinates, grows, and becomes a tree:

[45] This story, with some modifications, appears in various traditions.

if you understand these symbols,
you'll follow us, and fall to the ground, with us.[46]
(Rūmī)

[46] Translated by Nevit Ergin & C. Helminski, *The Rūmī Collection*, p. 90.

21

Sincerity

For the sincere. . .is an appointed nourishment
[*Sūrah Aṣ-Ṣaffāt* 37:40-41]

THE QUR'ĀN tells the story of Jesus عليه السلام who in his youth made birds out of clay. When he graced them with his breath, the birds came to life and flew away. The miracle was possible because Jesus breathed into the birds his heart's sincerity. Sincerity has the power to move heaven and earth.

Grandfather enjoyed unusual success in praying for rain showers to descend in areas of Northern Bengal where the lands were parched and scorched. His techniques were studied extensively by the serious and curious. People noticed that when he walked onto the lands and prayed for rain, his palms were turned downward. However, as he later explained, the technique of palms had nothing to do with the rains; in fact, he had no remembrance of his palms turning.

Two elements, he stressed, were of profound importance. Prior to the ritual of walking the lands and praying, he immersed himself in prayers, meditation, and fasting. Purification of the being was essential. Secondly, when praying for rain, he soaked his words in the deepest sincerity and humility. He found himself connecting with the vibration of an anguished cry pouring forth from the core of his being, from his soul, rising upwards higher and higher, begging, imploring for rain. And it was the sincerity of this anguished prayer from those mysterious depths, grandfather said, that at times opened up the heavens and brought down life-giving waters.

Spaciousness

Grandfather used the word "spaciousness" in explaining sincerity. There is sincerity of the personality and sincerity of the soul, depending on our spaciousness.

To religious fundamentalists who claimed sincerity in forcibly "helping" and "saving" others, grandfather told a simple story. There was a sincere monkey who insisted on rescuing fish from a neighborhood pond by plucking them out of the water in order to save them from a watery grave! This is an example of sincerity where spaciousness is limited.

As a person's personality becomes more aligned with the soul, the personality expands beyond its conditioned prejudices and imperfections. Such a person embodies spaciousness and is considered spiritually mature. The sincerity of such a being has heaven-like powers and is promised heavenly delights. The Qur'ān says that for the sincere "is an appointed nourishment: fruits and honor and dignity in gardens of felicity" [*Sūrah Aṣ-Ṣaffāt* 37:41-43].

Reflection

Sincerity is that whereby God is desired,
whatever the act may be.
(Junayd)[47]

Practices

Ask yourself:

- Do my words match my intentions?
- Do my actions reflect my beliefs?
- In presenting myself to others, is it my mask or my real face I am putting forward?

Sincerely and gently align yourself to the truth of who you really are. Your real face is beautiful; at your core, you are holy.

[47] A.J. Arberry, *Doctrine of the Sufis* (Cambridge, UK: University Press, 1978), p. 90.

22
Patience

Allāh is with those who patiently persevere
[*Sūrah Al-Baqarah* 2:153]

A *ḤADĪTH* remarks that patience is half of faith, a jewel among jewels. Patience is one of the most-frequently mentioned attributes of Allāh in the Qur'ān.

Two beggars knocked on the door asking for bread. One beggar was given a loaf and sent away. The other was kept waiting and waiting. At length, the second beggar became concerned. "Why am I being denied? What is so lacking in me that the other one was favored over me?" he asked himself. Unknown to the beggar, a fresh loaf was being baked for him inside the house.

The Qur'ān repeatedly invokes patience. In the face of obstacles and difficulties, the Prophet ﷺ is asked to be patient. If those who are unjust are allowed for a time to prosper, it is because God is patient. Humans are told to keep the faith and walk the path of justice and peace. Know that Allāh is with those who patiently persevere. "Wisdom and power follow endurance and patience," says a *ḥadīth.*

Patience has three components. The first is the art of mindfulness that asks you to be present with whatever is. Can you be like the hen sitting on the egg, present with the rhythms of nature?

The second component is a development of gentleness in yourself. Can you be less aggressive? Rushing ahead to clutch a floating feather will drive it further away. Turning on a powerful hose to fill up a small cup is an exercise in futility. But if you are present and gentle, the feather will be in your grasp and the cup will fill.

The third component, a most critical one, is the faith that there is a God who is infinitely Compassionate, Merciful, and Just; a God who is aware of our minutest needs and graciously provides.

A man stood before the saint Shiblī and said to him, "Which act of patience is hardest for one who is patient?"

Shiblī said, "Patience in God."

"No," the man said.

Shiblī said, "Patience for God."

"No," he said.

Shiblī grew angry and said, "Damn you, what then?"

The man said, "Patience without God Most High."

Shiblī let out a scream that nearly tore apart his spirit.

Although impatience can embroil us in difficulties and absurdities, it is wise to be compassionate with the impatience we feel in us. Grandfather put forth a charming hypothesis why we need to be gentle with ourselves. When impatient, we are possibly tapping into a subconscious memory of the time when we were in those divine realms before we arrived here. In those dimensions, whatever we thought of manifested instantly! On this plane of reality, we forget that we have to mature into higher states of being before any of that is possible. Thus, be gentle with yourself.

Reflection

The patience shown by the moon to the dark night
keeps it illumined;
the patience shown by the rose to the thorn
keeps it fragrant.[48]
(Rūmī)

[48] Mathnawī VI:1408, C. and K. Helminski, *Jewels of Remembrance*, p. 150.

23

Truthfulness

God is Ultimate Truth
[*Sūrah Al-Ḥajj* 22:6]

WHEN THE PROPHET MUḤAMMAD ﷺ preached that God is One, many Meccans were infuriated. In the beginning they ridiculed him. Then they made threats and later persecuted him. Because these methods failed, some prominent Meccans tried to bribe him. The Prophet declared: "Even if you put the Sun in my right hand and the Moon in my left hand, I shall never waver from the Truth."

Our souls have a passion for truth. Our aspiration for truth is God longing for God. A passionate commitment for truth is the way and the goal. Seeking truth is not about accumulating knowledge but about awakening to the heart of Reality—by living and becoming truth.

Islamic saints say there are three levels to awakening to truth. They use the metaphor of fire. The first level is to hear about fire; the second, to witness fire; and the third, to burn in the fire. The highest truth is that which we have experienced ourselves.

In the pursuit of truth, once again grandfather used the word spaciousness. Cultivate a sense of openness about your truth. Allow your truth to breathe. Don't suffocate it with your ego-hold. "Beware," grandfather cautioned, "you are not honoring truth; you are honoring your ego."

A disciple approached his teacher to give him exciting news. A non-Muslim with whom he had spent time was showing interest in converting to Islām. To his surprise, his teacher responded, "All this does is inflate your Islamic ego. Don't be so easily distracted. Focus on your real work."

To another student who was furious because someone criticized his religion, the teacher explained that Islām is as spacious as the sky. If someone spits at the sky, does it stain the sky? In fact, the spit returns to the person. It's not religion that is bruised but one's ego.

A favorite *ḥadīth* of Grandfather's, that he meditated on often and did his best to live, was as follows:

If a man gives up quarrelling when he is in the wrong,
A house will be built for him in Paradise.
But if a man gives up a conflict even when he is in the right,
A house will be built for him in the loftiest realm of Paradise.

Reflect upon the truth and live it. This pleases your Creator. The Qur'ān says, "Aren't you aware how God sets forth the likeness of a good word? It is firmly rooted like a good tree, its branches reaching toward the sky, yielding its fruit at all times by the permission of its Sustainer." [*Sūrah Ibrāhīm* 14:24-25].

Reflections

A conceited person sees someone sin,
and the flames of Hell rise up in him.
He calls that hellish pride defense of the Religion;
he doesn't notice his own arrogant soul.[49]
(Rūmī)

Practices

❖ Make a list of people to whom you have lied. Silently, in your mind, talk to them. Tell them the truth and from your heart ask for forgiveness. Then invoke God's mercy and forgive yourself.

[49] Ibid., Mathnawī I:3347-3348, p. 81.

FIVE PILLARS OF ISLAM

FIRST PILLAR: PROFESSION OF FAITH

Introduction to the Profession of Faith

There is no God but God
and Muḥammad is the Messenger of God

THE FIRST PILLAR of Islām is the creed of faith called the *Shahādah*. The exact words of the *Shahādah* are in two parts:

Lā ilāha ill Allāh;
Muḥammad ar Rasūl Allāh.

Literally, the words mean "There is no God but God; Muḥammad is the Messenger of God." The creed professes the unity of God and the prophethood of Muḥammad ﷺ.

The two-part *Shahādah* is filled with insights. It is useful to deal with each part separately.

24

The *Shahādah*—Part 1

There is no God but God

THIS VERSE affirming the unity of God is among the most repeated verses in the world, because it is recited by Muslims continuously. Upon the birth of a child the words of the *Shahādah* are tenderly spoken in the child's ears; on the person's death-bed, again, those words are said to him or her. Between birth and death that person's being becomes imprinted with the *Shahādah* in prayers, meditations, and in all occasions: joyous, tragic, unexpected, mundane, and special.

The understanding of this verse is encompassed by the heart, not the mind. One way to "perfume" our being with this insight is to meditate on sacred verses from the Holy Book. The Qur'ān, in a sense, is the best commentary upon itself: one part of the Qur'ān explains another. My parents chose the following verses for me to ponder, including one from Rūmī, to come closer to understanding the meaning of "There is no God but God":

- *Of knowledge we have given you but a little* [*Sūrah Al-Isrā'* 17:85].
- *Everywhere you turn is the face of Allāh* [*Sūrah Al-Baqarah* 2:115].
- *Since you have perceived the dust of forms, perceive the wind that moves them*[50] (Rūmī).
- *We are closer to you than your jugular vein* [*Sūrah Qāf* 50:16].
- *Everything that dwells upon the earth is perishing yet still abides the face of thy Lord, Majestic, Splendid* [*Sūrah Ar-Raḥmān* 55:26-27].

---

[50] Mathnawī VI:1460, translated by K. and C. Helminski, *The Rūmī Collection*, p. 70.

25

Mystery

Of knowledge we have given you but a little
[*Sūrah Al-Isrā᾿* 17:85]

IN SŪRAH 31, the Qur᾿ān says that if all the trees on earth were to become pens and the oceans ink, and after depletion, replenished by seven more oceans of ink, still this would not come close to fathoming God's mysteries [*Sūrah Luqmān* 31:27]. We are awash in mysteries within and without.

Indeed, of knowledge we have been given but a little. Here is Rūmī's advice: "Sell your cleverness and buy bewilderment! Cleverness is opinion, bewilderment vision."[51]

The Mystery of Existence

In the wee hours of the morning, the Mullah stumbled out of a tea-house and began wandering the street aimlessly. A policeman accosted him: "Who are you? Why are you out at this unusual hour? Where are you going?" "Sir," replied the Mullah. "If I knew the answer to all those questions, I would have been home a long time ago!"

Our deepest questions in life find resonance in sweet bewilderment. Rūmī muses:

Do you think I know what I'm doing?
That for one breath or half-breath I belong to myself?
As much as a pen knows what it's writing,

[51] Chittick, *The Sufi Path of Love*, p. 224.

or the ball can guess where it's going next.[52]

If we do not feel the sense of awe in us, it's because we are cooped up in the dark. Imagine, Rūmī asks, how it is to converse with an embryo cooped up in the dark. You might say, "The world outside is vast and intricate. There are wheat fields and mountain passes, and orchards in bloom. At night there are millions of galaxies, and in sunlight, the beauty of friends dancing at a wedding." Listen to the answer of the embryo: "There is no other world. I only know what I've experienced. You must be hallucinating."[53]

The Mystery of the Journey

Not only the thirsty seek the water,
the water as well seeks the thirsty.[54]
(Rūmī)

In a Mawlana Rūmī story, some sweet school-children urge their impoverished teacher to jump in the swollen flood waters and grab the bearskin coat floating by. The fur can keep the teacher warm in winter. He jumps in, grabs the coat, and then seems to have trouble bringing it out of the water. "Sir, dear teacher," plead the alarmed children, "Let go of the coat. Forget it. Please swim to shore quickly." "I've let go of it," shouts the teacher; "but it won't let go of me!" It was a live bear.[55] One of the more amazing things on our journey is that once you step on the path an invisible force like a magnet pulls and guides you.

This is how it is on the path. Something invisible gets hold of you and won't let go. Sooner or later, the Light hunts you down and dissolves the shadows in you as part of its own mysterious divine plan.

---

[52] Quatrain 1359, Barks and Moyne, *The Essential Rūmī,* p. 16.
[53] Ibid., Mathnawi III:49-62, pp. 70-71.
[54] Vaughan-Lee, *Travelling the Path of Love,* p. 56.
[55] K. Helminski, *The Rūmī Collection,* p. 88.

Grandfather cherished the insight of Bāyazīd Bisṭāmī that for thirty years he searched for God and came to the astonishing realization that God is the seeker and he, Bāyazīd, the one being sought! In fulfilling our life purpose, God's purpose is fulfilled.

And what is it like to experience that ultimate union with God that Islamic saints call *fanā*ᵓ (union with God) and *baqā*ᵓ (what subsists after union)? Grandfather invoked the ecstatic utterance of Kabir: "All know that the drop merges into the Ocean, but few know that the Ocean merges into the drop!"

The Mystery of the Hereafter

Our knowledge of the hereafter is limited by the human mind: what happens after death in those realms is a mystery. Vivid images describing heaven and hell in the Qurᵓān are metaphorical, meant to incline the heart of the believer to engage in "abiding good deeds" [*Sūrah Maryam* 19:76] and lessen our attachment to the "glittering show on earth" [*Sūrah Al-Kahf* 18:7]. Certainly we are accountable for our actions on earth, but the human understanding of rewards and punishment does not apply in those domains.

The Qurᵓān says, "To God belongs the secrets of the heavens and the earth" [*Sūrah Al-Kahf* 18:26]. Attempting to understand the invisible world with our sense faculties is as the village-saying goes: "Measuring the depth of the ocean with a bamboo stick."

Grandfather humbly offered his own understanding: on earth we are like schoolchildren learning and occasionally sitting for tests. In the hereafter we are given corrected answers and more learning. According to our level, our journey of evolving into perfection continues in heavenly spheres.

To convey the futility of trying to define the invisible worlds, grandfather enjoyed relating the following Rūmī story:[56]

A just king said to a dervish: "When total revelation has graced you,

[56] Thackston, *Signs of the Unseen*, p. 14.

and you come into the nearness of God, please remember me to God." The dervish answered, "When I step into that Presence and the Light of the Sun of Splendor shines over me, I will no more even remember myself. How do you expect me to remember you?"

ᶜAmal

Grandfather was some days of the month in a state of delicious daze. Some evenings he stayed up all night doing *ᶜamal*—a mystical practice where in a meditative state one continuously recites parts of the Qurʾān. Late into the night or early morning he felt palpably the presence of amazing energies. At times he saw incredible things. Sometimes he heard celestial music. Some specific invisible energies, grandfather said, became his allies in his work of healing. Joyously he proclaimed that he was a witness to a fraction of a fraction of the mysteries of the Universe. Grandfather was in total astonishment and felt unbounded gratitude!

If one drop of the Wine of Vision could rinse your eyes,
Wherever you looked, you would weep with wonder.[57]
(Rūmī)

Reflections

I have lived on the lip
of insanity, wanting to know reasons,
knocking on a door. It opens.
I've been knocking from the inside![58]
(Rūmī)

Observe the wonders as they occur around you.
Don't claim them. Feel the artistry

---

[57] Harvey, *Light Upon Light*, p. 96.
[58] Jalālu'ddin Rūmī, Furuzanfar #1249, *Unseen Rain*, translated by John Moyne and Coleman Barks (Putney, VT: Threshold Books, 1986), p. 75.

moving through, and be silent.[59]
(Rūmī)

Practices

- Practice sending light from your heart to the heart of every human soul you meet and, also, to the spirit of whatever you come in contact with: animals, trees, plants, flowers, water, stones, etc. This awakens and expands the Light in you.

---

[59] Mathnawī IV:3708-3709, Barks and Moyne, *The Essential Rūmī,* p. 153.

26

The Face of Allāh

Everywhere you turn is the face of Allāh
[*Sūrah Al-Baqarah* 2:115]

THE MULLAH traveled to the sacred Kaʿbah in the grand mosque of Mecca. After hours of prayer and meditation in the great mosque, the Mullah fell asleep. His feet pointed toward the Kaʿbah. This enraged some Meccans who woke him up and told him how disrespectful and sacrilegious it was to place his feet toward the House of Allāh. "Very well," said the Mullah, "please take my feet and put them in the direction where Allāh is not." The Meccans left the Mullah alone. "Everywhere you turn is the Face of Allāh," says the Qurʾān.

The Mud of Daily Existence

It follows, then, that this material world and activities we consider mundane are also the face of God. The Prophet Muḥammad ﷺ said, "Do not despise this world for this world, too, is from God."

In the East, the lotus flower is a symbol of beauty and spirituality. Notice, teachers tell us, that the flower has a stem that roots it in the mud. The spiritual flower owes its existence to the mud; it is the mud of daily existence that feeds the root of the spiritual flower. If we cannot find God in the mud of daily existence, how can we find God in some distant sacred place? Always, the face of Allāh is everywhere!

The Devil and the Face of Allāh

The Qurʾān says that the devil is a "slinking whisperer who whispers in the hearts of human beings" [*Sūrah An-Nās* 114:4-5]. Is the devil also the face of Allāh? Indeed, the devil is from God, but God does not approve of the devil. What is the meaning of this? This mystifying paradox is resolved only by higher consciousness. Mawlana Rūmī offers some examples for us to ponder on. A doctor for his or her livelihood needs people to become ill. Does a doctor approve of people suffering? A baker needs people to become hungry. Does a baker approve of them starving?

Through the mysterious presence of this "slinking whisperer," we develop qualities of restraint, discernment, right action, patience, and inner strength. Eventually, the energy of the devil is dissolved in the Light.

Closest to the Light

Regarding daily activities, a question commonly asked is this: how does one deal with the vast range of daily activities without getting overwhelmed? How do we make our lives sacred? One faces responsibilities with self, family, work, community, religion, etc. If the face of God is everywhere, how does one prioritize one activity over another?

Grandfather offered the following advice: "When unsure how to choose among all your activities, direct your effort on those closest to the Light." He derived this principle from a popular *ḥadīth* which says: "Make all your concerns one single concern and God will look after all your other concerns."[60]

Let's say, for example, that among some of your needs are raising money for your business, preparing for a lawsuit, attending a religious ceremony, and caring for your ailing mother. Ask yourself which of these is closest to the Light? Which activity holds the greatest sacredness and meaning for you? You decide on this by consulting with your inner teacher. Maybe you decide that taking care of your mother is closest to the Light. Willingly and lovingly, focus your activities on tending to her, and as for the others—the fundraising, the lawsuit, and the religious

[60] Fihi ma Fihi #49, quoting a ḥadīth, *The Rūmī Collection*, p. 61.

ceremony—give to them whatever is left of your energy and time without avoidance or aversion.

Again, you are asked not to use this formula as an excuse to avoid or delay working on that which is unpleasant or inconvenient to you. As you attend to what is closest to the Light, the others work themselves out wonderfully well. The Light, it is said, takes care of them. Islamic sages say that there is a great secret in this for anyone who can grasp it.

Reflections

Act for the present world
as if you were going to live forever
and act for the other world
as if you were going to die tomorrow.
(ᶜAlī ibn Abī Ṭālib [61] ﷜)

The business that veils me from the sight of your face
is the very essence of unemployment,
even though business may be its name.[62]
(Rūmī)

[61] These words were said by the Prophet's cousin, ᶜAlī ibn Abī Ṭālib. Some Islamic jurists say that he attributed these words to the Prophet ﷺ.
[62] Mathnawī VI:4423, C. and K. Helminski, *Jewels of Remembrance*, p. 189.

Larger Story

Since you have perceived the dust of forms,
perceive the wind that moves them.[63]
(Rūmī)

MOST OF US live and carry on upon the surface of the wondrous workings of Reality, remarkably unaware of the levels upon levels within which so much is going on.

Everything that happens in our lives is part of a larger story. Each situation has unknown elements to it. "We have shown you the dust but concealed the wind," says Rūmī.

The Qurʾān tells the story [*Sūrah Al-Kahf* 18:60-82] of Moses عليه السلام begging to accompany a being described as "one of our servants to whom we gave our mercy and whom we taught knowledge from our Presence" [*Sūrah Al-Kahf* 18:65]. Spiritual masters identify this being as Khiḍr عليه السلام, the "green one," a deathless prophet who over the centuries has appeared to those in genuine need of help. At first this nameless being is reluctant to have Moses accompany him, because Moses will not comprehend his doings. Later he yields on the understanding that Moses will not question his actions.

The esoteric prophet leads Moses عليه السلام on a journey and along the way damages a boat belonging to poor people, kills a youth, and repairs a wall in a town inhabited by rude and cruel people. In each episode Moses is disturbed and dumbfounded. He cannot help but protest in each instance. The deathless prophet proceeds to give an inner interpretation. In

---

[63] Mathnawī VI:1460, translated by K. and C. Helminski, *The Rūmī Collection*, p. 70.

the first case, a despotic king was seizing by force every ship but spared the ship belonging to the poor because it was temporarily crippled. In the second instance, the youth's life was snuffed out because "he would bring bitter grief upon his parents, who were true believers, by his overweening wickedness and denial of all truth" [*Sūrah Al-Kahf* 18:80]. In the third situation, there was a treasure underneath the wall belonging to orphans and the Lord wished that these orphans retrieve their buried inheritance upon reaching maturity. Each of these actions, explains the mysterious being, was "an act of mercy from your Lord" and "I did not act by my own command" [*Sūrah Al-Kahf* 18:82].

This, then, is a profound secret about circumstances and events in our lives: "Good or bad, only Allāh knows."

Reflections

Make no judgment in which there is no compassion.
(Traditional saying)

The servant of God is pleased with all that God does
in order that God may be pleased with all that he does.[64]
(Abū Saᶜīd ibn Abīʾl-Khayr)

Practices

Grandfather enjoyed sharing with everyone a simple but powerful practice called "sacred symbolism." Make your day-to-day activities part of a larger story. What is commonplace becomes sacred and meaningful.

- For instance, every time the Prophet Muḥammad ﷺ passed through any door, he paused to say, "Open to me the doors of Thy Mercy."
- When removing your clothing, you can say," I am peeling off layers of my ego."
- When showering: "These waters are cleansing and healing me physi-

[64] Vaughan-Lee, *Travelling the Path of Love*, p. 5.

cally, emotionally, and mentally."

- When talking on the phone: "The telephone is connecting me soul to soul to the other person."
- When shaking hands: "Through these hands, I transmit God's love and blessing."
- When driving a car: "May God's will steer me in the right direction in life."
- When falling asleep: "I surrender into the embrace of angels who transport me into celestial dimensions that nourish and nurture me."

28

Closeness

We are closer to you than your jugular vein
[*Sūrah Qāf* 50:16]

A WELL-KNOWN TEACHER was explaining to his students different ways to get close to God. He impressed on them the need for persistence: "You must keep knocking on the door with the faith that one day it will open to you." Rābiᶜa was passing by and heard his words. "When was the door ever closed?" she gently remarked. The teacher bowed to her.[65]

"He is with you wherever you are" [*Sūrah Al-Ḥadīd* 57:4] says the Qur'ān and "There are never three intimate conversation partners except that He is the fourth" [*Sūrah Al-Mujādalah* 58:7].

The paradox is that God is closer to us than our jugular vein and yet we feel so distant from Him. Kabir points out that "He is the breath inside the breath,"[66] but we search the world over to find Him. God is neither manifest nor hidden, revealed nor unrevealed, conscious nor unconscious. God is the ultimate mystery.

If I say He is within me,
the entire Universe hangs its head in shame;
yet if I say He is outside me,
I know I am a liar.[67]
(Kabir)

---

[65] Story by Attar, James Fadiman and Robert Frager, editors, *Essential Sufism*, edited by J. Fadiman and R. Frager (San Francisco, CA: Harper, 1997), p. 109.
[66] *The Kabir Book*, versions by Robert Bly (Boston, MA: Beacon Press, 1977), p. 33.
[67] Andrew Harvey and Eryk Hanut, *Perfume of the Desert* (Wheaton, IL: The Theosophical Publishing House, 1992), p. 41.

Words cannot describe and the mind cannot encompass this Absolute Reality. Allāh cannot be perceived directly, but through His attributes, ninety-nine of which are mentioned in the Qur'ān, He can be indirectly apprehended.

Even for beings as vast as prophets, the infinite space of God is overwhelming. Prophet Muḥammad ﷺ lamented, "We have not known You, O God, as You ought to be known."

The Prophet ﷺ lovingly revealed, however, that God longs for us to be close to Him. When we honor the abiding ache we have for Him and make an effort to come close to Him, our Creator responds most magnanimously. The *ḥadīth* says, "If my servant comes to Me walking, I go to him running."

The following story evoked for grandfather the mystery and beauty of Presence. A Bedouin was asked, "Do you acknowledge the Lord?" He replied, "How could I not acknowledge Him who has sent me hunger, made me naked and impoverished, and caused me to wander from country to country?" As he spoke thus, he entered into a state of ecstasy.

Reflections

In the name of Him Who has no name,
Who appears by whatever name you will call Him.[68]
(Dārā Shikoh)

By speech and by silence and by fragrance,
catch the scent of the King everywhere.[69]
(Rūmī)

The breath of the flute player,
does it belong to the flute?[70]
(Rūmī)

---

68 Vaughan-Lee, *Travelling the Path of Love*, p. 180.
69 Mathnawī III:981, C. and K. Helminski, *Jewels of Remembrance*, p. 8.
70 Mathnawī II:1793, C. and K. Helminski, *Rūmī Daylight*, p. 146.

Pleasure and Bliss

. . . yet still abides the Face of your Lord, Majestic, Splendid

THE QUR'ĀN says, "Everything that dwells upon the earth is perishing, yet still abides the Face of your Lord, Majestic, Splendid" [*Sūrah Ar-Raḥmān* 55:26-27]. We are asked to discern between form and essence and, ultimately, between pleasure and bliss. Can we set our hearts on that which is everlasting and not on that which is perishing?

> *Sunlight fell upon the wall;*
> *the wall received a borrowed splendor.*
> *Why set your heart on a piece of earth,*
> *O simple one? Seek out the source*
> *which shines forever.*[71]
> (Rūmī)

"Keep your heart awake,"[72] says Rūmī. Don't be deceived by the intoxication of the ego. Don't think all ecstasies are the same. Jesus عليه السلام was drunk with love for God; his donkey was drunk on barley.[73]

Heighten awareness and you will find, continues Rūmī, that the world is a magician and we are the merchants who buy yards of measured

---

[71] Ibid., Mathnawī II:708-709, p. 109.

[72] Andrew Harvey, *Teachings of Rūmī* (Boston, MA: Shambhala Publications, 1999), p. 36.

[73] Mathnawī IV:2691, C. and K. Helminski, *Jewels of Remembrance*, p. 78.

moonbeams.[74]

You are not being asked to forego or deny pleasure. Quite the contrary. You are being asked to move deeper beyond pleasure and come into bliss. Bliss is your birthright! You can have the entire Ocean; why are you so hung up on a drop of water? You can experience the mystery of galaxies; why are you so possessive of a dust particle? Seek Spirit! Move deeper into your experience of pleasure and always ask yourself, "Is this what I really want?" Be continuously mindful of what it is that you truly desire as you go through the desires of sex, food, wealth, and prestige. The truth is that within every desire of the created world is a secret yearning for something deeper that will not be satisfied until united with the formless.

Earthly flowers fade,
but the flowers that bloom from the heart—what a joy![75]
(Rūmī)

Grasp this truth in your heart and you will appreciate why a humble, aware person can happily share his loaf of bread and blanket with two others, whereas a king may have a realm and riches and yet scheme and plot to overcome the world.

Reflections

The prophets were not concerned with fame or bread.
Their only concern was to seek God's satisfaction,
and they acquired both fame and bread.
Whoever seeks God's satisfaction will be with the prophets
in this world and the next.[76]
(Rūmī)

[74] Mathnawi V:37-39, Moyne and Barks, *Open Secret*, p. 79.
[75] Mathnawī VI:4650, C. and K. Helminski, *Jewels of Remembrance*, p. 193.
[76] Fihi ma Fihi #49, *The Rūmī Collection*, p. 62.

Students of cunning have consumed their hearts
and learned only tricks;
They've thrown away real riches:
patience, self-sacrifice, generosity.[77]
(Rūmī)

Practices

- Whatever it is that your ego desires, ask yourself "Is this what I really want? Or is it something deeper?" When pursuing money or fame, ask yourself "Is it the money or title that I so anxiously want, or is it a desire for freedom or love?"
- In your wanting, when you connect to essence in place of appearance, many doors open up.

[77] Mathnawī II:3205-3206, C. and K. Helminski, *Rūmī Daylight*, p. 179.

30

The *Shahādah*—Part II

And Muḥammad is the Messenger of God

THE PROPHET MUḤAMMAD ﷺ is the conduit and repository of the miracle of Islām, the Qur'ān, a book of "Mercy and Guidance" [*Sūrah Luqmān* 31:3]. The Holy Book was transmitted through the person of the Prophet Muḥammad, who was illiterate. To accept Islām is to accept the Prophet through whom the message of the Qur'ān was delivered and who also was the embodiment of the message.

Muslims feel an exquisite affection and respect for the Prophet. Aware of every detail of his life, they are in sweet awe of how a human being was able to endure such enormous sadness and suffering with extraordinary grace, assume a bewildering variety of roles that were imposed on him, and accomplish so much in one lifetime.

Orphaned at the age of six, Muḥammad ﷺ found protection in the household of his grandfather and, later, with his uncle in a time-period described as an age of ignorance. Even as a child he had a mysterious and unrelenting belief in the oneness of God. As an adult, because of his refusal to stop preaching the Oneness of God, he was humiliated, harassed, and persecuted, all of which he bore with remarkable patience. Finally, in 622 A.D., he was forced to migrate (*hijrah*)[78] to Yathrib, renamed Medina (city of the Prophet). There he undertook and participated in an astounding variety of roles, among them: administrator, community

[78] The Prophet's custom of dating events from the *hijrah* was formalized by the Caliph ʿUmar; thus, the year of the *hijrah* became the first year of the Islamic era.

builder, political and military leader, mediator, judge, treaty maker, spiritual leader, and prophet. Within the space of ten years in Medina, the Prophet was able to reconcile centuries-long conflicts between various tribes and meld them into one community. In the same time-period, he was able to lay the groundwork for the spiritual flower of Islām to blossom and spread its fragrance in vast areas of the world. Muslims say this was possible because "God and his angels shower blessings upon the Prophet" [*Sūrah Al-Aḥzāb* 33:56]. How else could a human being in the face of severe obstacles, trials, and tribulations become a "lamp that gives light" [*Sūrah Al-Aḥzāb* 33:46] and a "bearer of good tidings and a warner for humankind" [*Sūrah Al-Aʿrāf* 7:188]?

Muslims delight in contemplating the words of the Prophet ﷺ (*ḥadīth*) as if "they were roses gathered in the skirt of one's robe."[79] They draw inspiration from the Prophet's conduct and life (*sunnah*), holding him in their minds as a model and exemplar. The Holy Book says that in the Prophet you have a "beautiful model of conduct" [*Sūrah Al-Aḥzāb* 33:21].

Mere Mortal

The Qur'ān reminds the Prophet ﷺ that he is a mere mortal. In one instance [*Sūrah ʿAbasa* 80:1-10], the Qur'ān admonishes the Prophet for ignoring a poor blind man who came to him for guidance. The Prophet was engaged at that time in explaining the oneness of God to an important tribal chieftain and had "frowned" on the imposition of the blind man. Yet the poor blind man was precious to God and the Prophet was rebuked for his lapse [*Sūrah ʿAbasa* 80:11].

The Qur'ān tells the Prophet ﷺ that there are innumerable prophets who came before him and there is "nothing revealed to you that has not been revealed to other apostles" [*Sūrah Fuṣṣilat* 41:43].

Jesus عليه السلام is described in the Qur'ān as the Spirit of God (*rūḥullāh*), Moses عليه السلام as one to whom God spoke (*kallamahullāh*), Abraham عليه السلام as

[79] Said by the Prophet's companions.

the Friend of God (*khalīlullāh*), and Muḥammad ﷺ as the Messenger of God (*rasūlullāh*). Muslims venerate all prophets who came before Muḥammad, but hold a special place in their hearts for the Prophet Muḥammad for three reasons.

First, here was a mortal who was completely human and yet completely immersed in the sacred. There is something unique about the way the Prophet ﷺ encompassed heaven and earth so completely.

Second, Muḥammad ﷺ, according to the Qur'ān, is the Seal of the Prophets: the last in a line of messengers through whom God sent revelations.

Third, and most important of all, the Qur'ān was transmitted through the person of the Prophet Muḥammad ﷺ.

Two Mystical Events

Islamic mystics rhapsodize over two mystical events in the Prophet Muḥammad's life ﷺ: the Night of Power (*Laylat al-Qadr*) and the Night of Ascent (*Laylat al-Miʿrāj*).

On the Night of Power, the first verses of the Qur'ān descended upon the Prophet ﷺ from the depths of Mystery in the stillness of the cave in Mecca. This extraordinary transmission from celestial realms continued for twenty-three years. Not only was the Qur'ān revealed, but Muḥammad was transformed into a Prophet.

The Qur'ān says of the process of Revelation, "Did we not expand your chest?" [*Sūrah Ash-Sharḥ* 94:1]. Islamic teachers say that this Qur'anic verse points to the essential work of seeking God's help in opening up our mind and heart in the journey of surrender.

Grandfather summarized some aspects of the Night of Power that he took to heart:

- The Qur'ān has its roots in the womb and mystery of silence.
- The verses of the Qur'ān were revealed little by little.
- The Qur'ān asks us to expand our mind and heart in the journey of surrender.

In the other mystical event, the Night Journey, the Prophet

Muḥammad ﷺ found himself transported from Mecca to Jerusalem. From there he ascended through seven levels of heaven. At the seventh level, the Prophet Muḥammad felt a deep yearning from his soul to ascend even higher so he could come closer to his Beloved. He paid attention to a voice inside of him and instantly he naughted every vestige of his ego, became love, and on the wings of love was able to complete his ascension. Grandfather focused on two aspects of the nocturnal journey of the Prophet:

- ❖ Only by experiencing true love are we able to ascend into our highest states.
- ❖ The horizontal and vertical journey suggests the importance of working equally in the visible and invisible realms.

In the following pages we shall touch upon some aspects of the Prophet Muḥammad's ﷺ two mystical events.

31

Silence

Through silence,
the Light of the beyond shines in our eyes.
(*Ḥadīth* of the Prophet Muḥammad ﷺ)

THE PROPHET MUḤAMMAD ﷺ, at a tender age, spent considerable periods in silence, despairing of the cruelty of his community. As an adult he retreated to caves in Mount Ḥirāʾ in Mecca, absorbed in meditation. Sometimes his wife, Khadījah ؓ, brought provisions and, together, they communed with the Mysteries for several days and nights at a time.

After many years of practicing meditation, at the age of forty, the Prophet ﷺ experienced a momentous encounter. The Angel Gabriel[80] appeared to the Prophet on the celebrated Night of Power (610 A.D.) and exclaimed, "*Iqraʾ!*" meaning "Recite!" Startled and shaken to the core, he mumbled that he was unlettered and could not read or write. "*Iqraʾ!*" came back the command, "Proclaim in the name of your Lord who is the Creator and Cherisher of all!" [*Sūrah Al-ʿAlaq* 96:1].

Filled with awe and terror, thinking he had gone mad and was hallucinating, he ran down the mountain and sought comfort and assurance from his beloved wife, Khadījah ؓ. She lovingly assured him of his sanity and, after consulting with a blind seer, she encouraged him to return to the mountain.

The Prophet Muḥammad ﷺ returned and, again, the angel appeared. He felt an intense crushing embrace and suddenly he heard words

[80] In Arabic, *Jibrīl* or *Jibrail* is literally "God's Mighty One." In Islamic cosmology, he is one of the Archangels and the Angel of Revelation.

of startling beauty and sacredness.

This astonishing transmission from the depths of Mystery continued for twenty-three years. Often the words came unexpectedly and, sometimes, in response to a question. The words were seared into the Prophet's ﷺ memory and he repeated them to family and friends who inscribed them onto the bark of trees, parchments, stones, etc. The compilations of these sacred words is now known as the Qur'ān. The Qur'ān has its roots in the mystery of Silence.

How amazing is the mystery of Silence! All things are born from and die in the arms of an infinite Silence which is variously named. Spiritual teachers call it *Kibriya*, the golden bed of Silence from where all the rose gardens of the world flower and into which they fade.

The Practice of Silence

We suffocate when we get too caught up in this world. We are like fish out of water, thrashing and quivering on shore; we need to dive into those life-giving waters from time to time.

This inner state has to be experienced. Words cannot convey the phenomenal grace of silence.

Now be silent.
Let the One who creates the words speak.
He made the door.
He made the lock.
He also made the key.[81]
(Rūmī)

Silence as a spiritual practice is simple but not easy. Grandfather emphasized two points about the practice of silence. First, cultivate a sense of intuitive balance in your contemplation. The Qur'ān offers guidance on the proper state of meditation:

---

[81] Jalālu'ddin Rūm, Ode 2820, *Rūmī - In the Arms of the Beloved*, translated by Jonathan Star (NYC, NY: Jeremy P. Tarcher/ Putnam, 1997), p. 29.

His gaze did not turn aside, nor go too far
He had seen signs of His Lord, great signs.
[*Sūrah An-Najm* 53:17-18]

Of great significance is the "gaze" of the Prophet ﷺ that does not "turn aside" or "go too far." This evolving sense of balance comes with awareness and experience.

Second, persist with the practice. Grandfather remarked that there are many who sing praises of this practice but few who regularly practice silence. An underlying feeling is that, yes, the benefits are great, but they don't last long. You feel content and peaceful for a while but once you return to the turbulence of day-to-day reality, you are back to your old, anxious, conditioned self. Of what use is the practice of silence if the benefits dissipate?

The reality is that with regular practice of silence, slowly something opens and deepens in you and eventually this state abides and endures. Then, when you face reality, you experience equanimity: a sense of centeredness, peaceful and present with whatever comes and goes.

Grandfather used a metaphor to explain how the process worked. Dip your shirt in a vat filled with dye and you will find that the color on the shirt lasts a little while and then fades away. But keep dipping the shirt in the vat repeatedly and after a time the color becomes permanent. The shirt is now colorfast! Similarly, as you keep immersing your being in the vat of God-consciousness through the practice of silence, at one point in time the fragrance of Divine attributes perfumes your being permanently. As some like to say, the Blush of the Beloved abides in you.

Silence, in its pristine dignity and mystery, simply is. It does not need to clamor for our attention or bemoan its absence. Wordless, unfathomable, it awaits.

A skeptic approached Mawlana Rūmī and said, "If you believe in silence, why have you talked and talked?" The Master laughed and said lovingly, "The most Radiant One in me has not said one word!"

Anjuman-e-Khamoshi

Students of grandfather and children in the village loved to hear stories of *Anjuman-e-Khamoshi* (Persian for "the Society of Silence"). This centuries-old secret circle was a community of highly evolved teachers who, collectively, through their silent presence and intentions, deepened vibrations of peace, love, and good will around the world. All communications between these advanced beings were sent and received through the mystery of silence. The only times the circle met in Baghdad were for the ritual of initiating new members.

A popular story about the twelfth-century Master ᶜAbdul Qādir Jīlānī says he proceeded to Baghdad to be inducted as a new member. He had intuited that a member of the Circle had passed away and there was space for him.

Before Jīlānī arrived in Baghdad, the Circle had accepted another sage into their ranks. An emissary was sent to meet with Jīlānī outside the gates of Baghdad to convey this news.

The emissary brought with him a glass and a pitcher of water. In silence the emissary poured water into the glass, filling it to the brim, indicating fullness. The master paused, moved his hands and plucked a rose petal from thin air. He put the petal on the water. His actions symbolized two things: he had achieved a state where he could materialize the petal out of nowhere, and the petal on the water did not disturb its fullness.

Immediately the gates of Baghdad swung open. Members of the circle rushed out to greet its newest member, in silence of course. Ever since this episode, Master Jīlānī has been called "The Rose of Baghdad."

Reflections

Keep silent in order to hear God's whisper.[82]

(Rūmī)

---

[82] Jalālu'ddin Rūmī, Dīwān Ode 233, *Breathing Truth*, translated by Muriel Maufroy (London, England: Sanyar Press, 1997), p. 241.

Keep silent, bathe in this wonder.
Renounce the secrets: this is the Secret.[83]
(Rūmī)

[83] Ibid., p. 234.

32

Little by Little

So . . . we may strengthen your heart
[*Sūrah Al-Furqān* 25:32]

THE QUR'ĀN was revealed over a period of twenty-three years. It was sent down, little by little, stage by stage, in order that it might "strengthen the heart."

Rūmī says that deep in the earth, ordinary stones are becoming rubies gradually. An ordinary stick breaks into a bud imperceptibly. We flower into the fullness of our being little by little.

There is sacredness in the words "little by little." God could have sent full-blown perfect beings, flying through the cosmos, to arrive here in one instant. Gradualness, it seems, is favored by that mysterious Intelligence.

The marvelous creation of a child takes nine months. A great task is often accomplished by a series of small acts. A skillful cook lets the pot boil slowly. Night by night the new moon gives a lesson in gradualness. The Qur'ān says that "God's only command when willing anything is saying to it, 'Be!'—and it is" [*Sūrah Yā Sīn* 36:82]. But even the Universe took a few days to be in place! Gradualness, indeed, is a characteristic of the action of the Sustainer of the Universe.

Do your work of transformation little by little. Rūmī says: "Little by little, wean yourself. This is the gist of what I have to say. From an embryo, whose nourishment comes through the blood, move to an infant drinking milk, to a child on solid food, to a searcher after wisdom, to a hunter of more invisible game." [84]

Grandfather said that by doing the work of inner growth, little by little you make progress, increment by increment, and, suddenly there is a big jump. You come back to increment by increment and again, a big jump! The big jump happens because of the little-by-little application. It's a law. Truly, it pays to persist, little by little.

Grandfather enjoyed telling the following story. The Mullah was enamored of Indian classical music. He eagerly sought out a teacher to take private lessons. "How much will it cost?" asked the Mullah.

"Three pieces of silver the first month and one piece of silver from the second month onwards," replied the teacher.

"Excellent!" replied the Mullah, "Sign me up from the second month!"

---

[84] Mathnawi III:49-62, Barks and Moyne, *The Essential Rūmī,* pp. 70-71.

33

Open Mind

"O Lord, make me see things as they really are"
(*Ḥādith* of the Prophet Muḥammad ﷺ)

AFTER THE PROPHET'S ﷺ amazing experience with the Angel Gabriel, a spontaneous prayer bubbled up from within him. Daily the Prophet asked of God, "O Lord, make me see things as they really are."

The truth is that Reality does not touch our minds directly but through the perceptual filters of beliefs and concepts. Until we practice awareness, we cannot begin to gauge the conditionings imposed on our mind that lead to biases, judgments, and habitual patterns of thinking.

How does one open the mind?

One way is to expand our knowledge and so have an ever-widening vision. The very first revelation of the Qur'ān says, "We taught man the use of the pen" [*Sūrah Al-ʿAlaq* 96:4]. One *ḥādith* encourages human beings to "seek knowledge from cradle to grave," and another to travel far and wide in quest of knowledge "even as far as China." To deepen our understanding of God's creation is a sacred task.

Second, an open mind means to have a readiness and ability to admit to oneself, and if need be to others, that one is mistaken. The Prophet Muḥammad ﷺ once observed some date palm growers doing a particular type of grafting. He advised them against it. The farmers enthusiastically followed his counsel but suffered a significant decline in yield. When the Prophet learned about this, he admitted his error and apologized saying, "I am a mere human being." He advised them to listen to him when it came to learning about revelations which came from God, but when it came to worldly matters, to bear in mind that he was a mere mortal.

This willingness to admit one's mistakes creates spaciousness in the mind to hold deeper truths. Otherwise we are busy forcing everything to fit our truth.

The Mullah was employed in the royal palace, and there for the first time he saw a royal falcon. "What a strange looking pigeon!" the Mullah thought to himself. Eager to be of service, he took out a clipper and trimmed the claws, wings, and beak of the falcon. "And now, finally," remarked the Mullah with satisfaction, "You look like a decent pigeon. Obviously, your keeper had been neglecting you!"

Third, opening the mind means giving oneself permission to look at whatever comes our way. The Qur᾽ān suggests that nothing in our life is an isolated accident. Every event, circumstance, or relationship has a meaning and purpose. Can we acknowledge every aspect and situation in our life? Can we be mindful of the tendency to avoid or deny that which is inconvenient or unpleasant? Islamic psychologists are in full agreement with Carl Jung when he says that those aspects of ourselves that we deny or repress are having their stories rendered unheard or unseen. Inevitably, they will rise and revolt. It is important to shine the light of awareness onto the shadows in our lives. Under the persistent light of consciousness, little by little and always with compassion for oneself, the shadows are transformed.

There's bankruptcy that's pure gain.
The moon stays bright when it
doesn't avoid the night.[85]
(Rūmī)

Fourth, can we choose to dwell on images and feelings that are life-affirming? Often we are not aware of our thoughts or are unwilling to look at them. We risk sinking into places where unconsciously we build negative and imaginary scenarios with accompanying negative feelings.

[85] Barks, *Birdsong*, p. 33.

This unconscious and pessimistic build-up can overwhelm us. The moment we become aware of this negativity swirling up in us, we need to immediately and urgently talk to ourselves. We need to tell ourselves, "Stop! Pay attention! This is not real! Not real!" Immediately invoke prayers and sacred recitations seeking refuge in the Infinite Compassion and Bounty of God. This creates sacred vibrations that transform negativity.

Become aware of the power of thought and especially the resulting images and feelings we habitually linger on.

If your thought is a rose,
you are *a rose garden;*
if it is a thorn,
you are fuel for the bath stove.[86]
(Rūmī)

Baan

In grandfather's village of Mahdipur, villagers have a sophisticated understanding of the power of negative thoughts. They are sensitive to and actually scared of a ritual called *baan*, loosely translated as a curse. If someone is obsessed with hurting another, that person focuses intensely on hateful thoughts and, in a prolonged ritual, combines feelings with visualizations, recitations, and intentions. Negative thoughts congeal into powerful energy-forms that are used by the mind as projectiles to hurt another. The sender almost always comes to a sorry end, drained and consumed by negativity. What is sometimes surprising is that the consequences for the recipient can be devastating if he or she is not spiritually protected. Doctors are amazed to find patients in the village physically wasting away even though there is no medical cause for this deterioration.

Grandfather taught simple heartfelt prayers and recitations. He ex-

[86] Mathnawī II:278, C. and K. Helminski, *Rūmī Daylight*, p. 100.

plained that by invoking them we create life-affirming vibrations. By seeking refuge in God, we dissolve the effects of negativity and rest in Divine protection and love. He asked his students to memorize and reflect on *Sūrah Al-Falaq,* which is a protection against negative forces. The Qur'ān advises: "Say, I take refuge with the Lord of the Dawn. . . . From the mischief of those who practice secret arts and from the mischief of the envious one as he practices envy" [*Sūrah Al-Falaq* 113:1, 4-5].

34

Open Heart

". . . but I can be contained in the heart of my loving servant"

IN A *ḤADĪTH* QUDSĪ, Allāh says:

I cannot be contained in the space of the earth
I cannot be contained in the space of the heavens
But I can be contained in the heart of my loving servant.

The Divine Heart, we are told, is in the human heart. Between heart and Heart lie level upon level of consciousness and realization. A man or woman's innermost meaning is in the heart. To open our heart is to experience our vastness and be filled with spiritual vision. True knowing is from the heart. The Qur'ān says "the heart in no way falsified what it saw" [*Sūrah An-Najm* 53:11].

Rūmī, astonished by the transformation of his being, uttered:

Close down speech's door and open up the heart's window!
The Moon will only kiss you through the window.[87]

To Know the Heart is to Experience the Heart

How does one open up the heart? There are the beautiful practices of purifying the heart and cultivating stillness. But the basic step is to give ourselves permission to experience feelings that come up in our life, al-

[87] Furuzanfar #19863, Chittick, *The Sufi Path of Love*, p. 38.

ways with compassion for oneself. Can we embrace our ten thousand joys of life as well as our ten thousand sorrows? To know the heart is to experience the heart.

Sacred Trembling

If feelings are the passageway from heart to Heart, why do we run away from feelings? Because we fear the pain of what grandfather called "sacred trembling." We dread trembling with our feelings of sadness, grief, jealousy, or other pains. Trembling means that you allow yourself to be present with these feeling sensations. To what extreme lengths we go to build a complex of armor and stone walls around the heart—anything to avoid pain! Paradoxically, the closed heart increases pain and stifles any potential for joy. The sweet irony is that it is in the trembling that the pain softens.

Even more fascinating is that in the process of trembling, pain gives way to transformation. Trembling is severe and awesome but as you tremble, the pain softens and this is the process by which "the locks on their hearts" [*Sūrah Muḥammad* 47:24] open up. With this unlocking, amazing things happen:

Something opens our wings. Something
makes boredom and hurt disappear.
Someone fills the cup in front of us:
We taste only sacredness.[88]
(Rūmī)

Have you not noticed, says Mawlana Rūmī, that fruits do not grow on the trunks of trees? To receive the divine blush, the soul of the fruits needs to tremble and quiver in the breeze.

Don't be scared to tremble with your feelings. When you go through a deep dark forest, half the time you are going in, the other half you are coming out! It's your passageway to the Divine Heart. The jour-

---

[88] Furuzanfar #1084, Moyne and Barks, *Unseen Rain*, p. 56.

ney is sacred.

Spiritual teachers offer this insight: "The way beyond is through." You can jump above, around, or creep underneath this dread sensation, but sooner or later you realize you have to go through it.

Grandfather went to some lengths to emphasize that only when you take the trembling steps with compassion for yourself, does the trembling become sacred.

The other point he underlined is that there is no need to rush through the feeling. Take the trembling steps little by little.

Holdings in the Body

When one is mindful of feelings, one becomes aware that feelings register as physical sensations in the body. No matter how we label the emotions or feelings, they are experienced in the body. The heart was placed in the body for a reason; the body makes us aware of what needs our attention and our love. We have the opportunity to greet the sensations with awareness and compassion. The process of acknowledging and honoring the sensations in the body brings us closer and closer to the Divine Heart.

Feelings are energies; feelings that come up are begging for our attention. Ignore them and they will return again and again to haunt you. Reject them and you have missed out on the opportunity for growth. Thus, a simple disagreement between two friends is not so much a disagreement but aspects of each surfacing in order to be healed and integrated. The feelings that come up are exactly what each person needs for healing and empowerment.

Does this mean that we seek out and entice pain to come into our lives because it has lessons to teach us? Of course not! Another insight from the wise: "Don't run towards pain; just don't run away from it."

The dark thought, the shame, the malice,
meet them at the door laughing,
and invite them in.

Be grateful for whoever comes,
because each has been sent
as a guide from beyond.[89]
(Rūmī)

Such is the beauty of transformation in human beings that even angels, we are told, are jealous! Angels have no physical bodies and so do not suffer the anguish of painful sensations. They are in awe of humans who receive the sensations with awareness and who, with compassion, little by little, metamorphize their beings.

From those mysterious depths, Rūmī heard a divine whisper:

There is no angel so sublime, He whispered
Who can be granted for one moment
What is granted you forever.
And I hung my head, astounded![90]
(Rūmī)

Tears

When the heart opens and tears flow, what a blessing! These waters are holy. They invite Divine Presence.

Wherever water falls, life flourishes.
Wherever tears fall, Divine mercy is shown.[91]
(Rūmī)

Grandparents constantly said that tears that stream from the wellsprings of one's being water apple orchards and rose gardens in the invisible world. So, as Rūmī says, "Weep like the waterwheel, that green herbs may spring up from the courtyard of your soul."[92]

---

[89] Mathnawī V:3693-95, Barks and Moyne, *The Essential Rūmī,* p. 109.
[90] Harvey, *Light Upon Light,* p. 6.
[91] Mathnawī I:820, C. and K. Helminski, *Rūmī Daylight,* p. 32.
[92] Ibid., Mathnawī I:821, p. 32.

Note that spiritual teachers are talking about tears that surge from the depths of one's being, not the lamentations and tears that arise from a need for attention, the melodrama of the personality. The latter is a form of attachment that does not allow us to move deeper to reach the laughter hidden in tears, the treasure amid the ruins. To open the heart, we have to keep moving into deeper spaces. We lose out if we remain stuck.

Honor your sadness by feeling the sensations. Tremble with your tears and move closer toward your core. At the core of your sadness is enduring joy and bliss.

But listen to me: for one moment,
quit being sad. Hear blessings
dropping their blossoms
around you. God.[93]
(Rūmī)

Reflections

In the heart of man lies the Throne of the All-Merciful.
(*Ḥadīth Qudsī*, spoken through the Prophet Muḥammad ﷺ)

He has afflicted you from every direction
in order to pull you back to the Directionless.[94]
(Rūmī)

If you are irritated by every rub,
How will your mirror be polished?[95]
(Rūmī)

---

[93] Furuzanfar #2738, Barks and Moyne, *The Essential Rūmī*, p. 8.
[94] Furuzanfar #3952, Chittick, *The Sufi Path of Love*, p. 238.
[95] Mathnawī I:2980, C. and K. Helminski, *Rūmī Daylight*, p. 69.

I saw grief drinking a cup of sorrow
and called out,
"It tastes sweet,
does it not?"
"You've caught me,"
grief answered,
"and you've ruined my business.
How can I sell sorrow,
when you know it's a blessing?"[96]
(Rūmī)

Practices

Sacred Holding:

Sacred holding is an ancient technique. Grandfather said that the Prophet Muḥammad ﷺ practiced this for many years in the silence and mystery of the Meccan caves.

Grandfather impressed upon his students that sacred holding is a supremely powerful technique meant to be practiced for a lifetime. When negative feelings come up in you, take time to do this exercise at the earliest opportunity.

- The first step is to allow yourself to experience. Tell yourself that every feeling is valid. Ask yourself, "What feeling is coming up in me?" Name that feeling. Maybe it is anger, sadness, jealousy, or bitterness.
- In the second step, ask yourself, "Where do I hold this feeling in my body? Locate the feeling. It definitely has a resting place in your body. We are able to experience a feeling because it registers as a physical sensation somewhere in the body.
- In the third and very important step, receive this "holding" in your body with compassion for yourself. Encompass the physical sensa-

[96] Barks, *Birdsong*, p. 19.

tions in your body with the embrace of your soul. From your heart, send love and mercy to this physical holding. Talk tenderly to yourself; cultivate a gentle rapport with yourself. Tell yourself, for example, "I'm sorry you feel this. . . . This is difficult. . . . Let me tenderly support you. . . ." At this time there is no need to fix or analyze the sensations, simply a need to be present with the holding for as long as you want. This is the process of trembling.

❖ In the fourth step, focus gently on the holding in your body and intend to inhale and exhale through that part of you. Allow divine breath to caress you there.

These four steps acknowledge, nurture, and integrate those feelings in God's Light. Slowly, as you persist with this technique, an amazing shift occurs: that which was negative, irksome, and painful, integrates and now transforms into a source of strength and wholeness in you.

Because sacred holding encompasses all feelings, it is possible to do this practice with positive feelings that come up in you. Tremble with the feelings and express gratitude in your heart for the blessing.

In the moments that you open up to the joys and sorrows of life, the gateway to the heart opens.

35
Love

Out of love, Allāh made His Bounties flow to you

IN THE QURʾĀN, Allāh is *Al-Wadūd*, the One who Loves. It is out of love that "Allāh has made in service to you all that is in the heavens and on earth and made His Bounties flow to you in abundant measure, seen and unseen" [*Sūrah Luqmān* 31:20]. Love is the cause and essence of everything.

The Universe coheres because of love. Love turns the wheels of heaven. It is for lovers that the spheres turn and turn. Ecstatic love is an Ocean, and the Milky Way just the foam floating on it.[97]

On some level, minerals, plants, and animals live and die for love.

grass agrees to die
so that it can rise up and receive
a little of the animal's enthusiasm[98]
(Rūmī)

How little we know of love! Rūmī says, "No matter what I say to explain and elucidate Love, shame overcomes me when I come to Love itself."[99] We experience love as subtle degrees of domination and servitude. But this is not love! Rūmī proclaims:

---

[97] Jalālu'ddin Rūm, *Poems of Rūmī*, translated by Robert Bly and Coleman Barks (S. San Francisco, CA: Audio Literature, 1989).
[98] Ibid.
[99] Mathnawī I:112, Chittick, *The Sufi Path of Love*, p. 194.

but love is different
it arrives complete
just there
like the moon in the window . . .
love is the sea of not-being
and there intellect drowns . . .
this is the shoreless sea;
here swimming ends
always in drowning.[100]

The garden of love is green without limit
and yields many fruits other than sorrow or joy.
Love is beyond either condition:
without spring, without autumn, it is always fresh.[101]
(Rūmī)

There is a Kiss We Want

Rūmī says, "There is some kiss we want with our whole lives, the touch of spirit on the body."[102] We yearn to kiss and be kissed by the Beloved. We have within us an unquenchable love thirst.

Allow yourself to be drawn by the stronger pull of what you really love and astonishing truths will be revealed to you. Keep moving and come into the essence of what you truly love. The Beloved, you will find, is the source of all Love. We are shadows in love with the Sun. The Sun comes up and the shadows are quickly naughted. Until we come to the Essence, our love feels incomplete. The mystic Kabir asks, "Who is it we spend our entire life loving?"[103] All desires are really for that Absolute Mystery, obscure and veiled.

---

[100] Translated by D. Liebert, *The Rūmī Collection*, p. 48.
[101] Ibid., Mathnawī I:1793-1794, translated by K. Helminski, p. 195.
[102] Jalālu'ddin Rūmī, Furuzanfar 1888, *The Soul of Rūmī,* versions by Coleman Barks (New York, NY: HarperCollins, 2001), p. 127.
[103] Bly, *The Kabir Book*, p. 27.

It is He who suffers His absence in me,
Who through me cries out to Himself.
Love's most strange, holy mystery –
We are intimate beyond belief.[104]
(Rūmī)

Ultimate Love

A much-loved topic of grandfather's was to talk about the meaning of Ultimate Love, which is about loving God, the love that truly satisfies and fulfills. He was very mindful of the human tendency to separate the love of God from love of others. He observed in himself and others that one might pray, meditate, and express love for God, but when it came to dealings with strangers, neighbors, the poor, and in the treatment of animals, one might sometimes be inconsiderate, indifferent, even cruel. Grandfather had a clear understanding that loving God is simply about deepening the capacity within to hold love for God.

You cannot just keep saying, "O God, I love you so much," and expect to be fulfilled. You have to deepen and widen the spaciousness within you to hold that enormous love. The absolute Splendor of the Beloved and the capacity within us to hold love for the Beloved are revealed as one and the same. This insight is at the heart of Ultimate Love.

How do you deepen the inner capacity to love? According to Grandfather, this lifelong process is twofold: loving oneself continuously and loving the creation of the Beloved—one's fellow beings, the animal, vegetable, and mineral kingdoms, all that is of God.

By loving yourself, you expand the capacity within to hold love for others. You become aware that all outer relationships are a reflection of the inner relationship you have with yourself. How you bond with yourself is how you will bond with others; how you love yourself is how you will love others.

The minute I heard my first love story,

---

[104] Vaughan-Lee, *Travelling the Path of Love*, p. 59.

I started looking for you, not knowing
how blind that was.

Lovers don't finally meet somewhere.
They're in each other all along.[105]
(Rūmī)

With an increased capacity to love, one knows at a deep level that one cannot love God without loving God's creation. To love and serve God's creation is to love and serve the Creator.

In a *ḥadīth qudsī,* God asks the son of Adam ﷺ, "Why did you not visit Me when I was ill?" The human being is dumbfounded and in a daze. He stutters, "You are the Lord of the Worlds!" God then explains that when one of His servants is unwell, "you will find Me with him." When food and drink are offered to him, they are offered to Him also.

With exquisite tenderness mystics plead that no matter how many times you are rejected or hurt, please keep moving deeper into love. In all your relationships, can you love with a sense of joy, sacredness, and commitment? Don't ever give up on love!

If you do righteous deeds and have loved faithfully, the Qur'ān promises that you will be brought in the end into the presence of Supreme Love itself—"the Compassionate will endow with Love" [*Sūrah Maryam* 19:96]. You will be graced and blessed by the Love that truly satisfies.

I am drunk on the wine of the Divine Majesty.
The thought of a final Beauty leaps like a deer in my heart
Like the moon racing up the sky, like a lily
Lifting its head suddenly from the river grass.[106]
(Rūmī)

---

[105] Furuzanfar 1246, Moyne and Barks, *Open Secret,* p. 19.
[106] Harvey, *Light Upon Light,* pp. 185-186.

Reflections

You will not enter Paradise until you love one another.
(*Ḥadīth* of the Prophet Muḥammad ﷺ)

O God, Grace me with love of You and to love those who love you and to love whatever brings me nearer to You.
(A prayer of the Prophet Muḥammad ﷺ)

I cried, "The drunken heart, where is it going?"
"Be silent," the King of kings answered,
"It is coming towards Us."[107]
(Rūmī)

That which God said to the rose
and caused it to laugh in full blown beauty,
He said it to my heart
and made it a hundred times more beautiful.[108]
(Rūmī)

Practices

Adoring the Heart:

Grandfather delighted in a meditative practice that he called the sacred technique of adoring the heart. He felt a special need to share this technique with as many people as possible.

- ❖ With eyes closed, in a state of meditation, focus on your heart; rest your attention on the heart space. Softly, and with tenderness, tell your heart repeatedly: "I love you . . . I love you so much . . . I really love you." Say the words with as much feel-

[107] Maufroy, *Breathing Truth*, p. 122.
[108] Mathnawī III:4129, Kabir E. Helminski, *The Knowing Heart* (Boston, MA: Shambhala Publications, 1999), p. 89.

ing as you can evoke. If the words do not resonate, change to: "I am willing to love you." If for some reason the word love does not feel right at this time, substitute with another word like "cherish" or "honor." Say the words to your heart again and again no matter how awkward it feels. Your ego might resist, so persist! Eventually, the ego lets go, for in the face of genuine, abiding love, the ego is helpless. With continuous practice, a supremely healing and empowering vibration goes from the tongue into the mouth, into the throat, the chest, then deep into the heart, and from there inside the soul, into the hidden, then into the hidden of the hidden.

Do this practice daily and experience the mystery of love unfolding in you with life-changing consequences.

36

Two Realms

Work equally in visible and invisible realms

THE NIGHT JOURNEY or *Miʿrāj* of the Prophet Muḥammad ﷺ has enchanted Muslims everywhere. Wrapped in meditation and prayer, the Prophet, to his astonishment, found himself in a vision transported horizontally on a divine winged steed called Burāq,[109] from Mecca to Jerusalem. There, accompanied by the Angel Gabriel, he ascended vertically through seven levels of heaven. He came into the indescribable and unspeakable nearness of Divinity.

To grandfather, the powerful symbolism of the *Miʿrāj* is that the work of inner transformation is twofold: horizontal and vertical. Call it "working in the visible and invisible worlds." We are asked to work equally in both worlds.

Working in the visible world means that we participate fully in the bazaar of life: buying, selling, marrying, raising children, etc. We are asked to become aware of our hour-to-hour, day-to-day issues that come up in our lives as we interact with family, friends, work, and community. The work involves bringing the light of awareness to gently shine on the shadows that come up in our relationships and interactions. Can we acknowledge these elements in our personality, deal with them, and work

---

[109] In Islamic tradition, this miraculous winged horse-like creature was the mount of the Prophet Muḥammad on his night journey. Burāq derives from *baraqa*, which means to "glitter," as in lightning. During the Prophet's night journey, Burāq proceeded in flashes of speed. Wherever Burāq's glance landed, the next bound brought it there. Burāq is also a metaphor for Intellect, a "knowing" without the process of analysis.

through them to become more mature ourselves?

Working in the invisible realm means cultivating practices that expand and nourish our being. From time to time we need to dive into those life-giving waters—silence, meditation, prayer, nature, music, sunsets, laughter—anything that connects us to the vast mystery we are immersed in. The Qurʾān says that everything in the visible world has its roots in the invisible world. Water those invisible roots from time to time.

Non-existence is the place of income;
don't run away from it.
This existence of more and less,
is the place where we spend.[110]
(Rūmī)

For inner growth we need to work in both worlds. If you insist on working only in the visible world, because you are a realist, then you are nothing more than a "wretched employee." The best you can do is to reach the frontiers of your personality and manage a life of "quiet desperation."

If you work only in the invisible world and avoid issues that come up in you as you relate to family, community, and society in the visible world, then you are avoiding the actuality of your own life. Why are you here?

When doing the work in the visible and invisible realms, be aware that the two dimensions carry different loads. Do not substitute one for the other just because it seems more convenient. Rūmī points out that too often we put the saddlebags on Jesus عليه السلام and let the donkey run loose in the pasture.[111] If you had an examination to pass, and instead of studying, you prayed, meditated, and made hourly offerings to God, do you think that angels would write the examination for you? Pray de-

---

[110] Mathnawī II:689, C. and K. Helminski, *Rūmī Daylight,* p. 108.
[111] Mathnawi V:1094, Barks and Moyne, *The Essential Rūmī,* p. 256.

voutly, but also study devoutly. The Prophet ﷺ said, "Trust in Allāh, but tether your camel first."

Grandfather personified in his work of healing the need to work in visible and invisible worlds. With a patient, typically he made a physical diagnosis and prescribed herbal medicine. This was only one half. For the other half he worked in the invisible world in various ways: uttering Qur'anic verses over an amulet which he advised the patient to wear, reciting Qur'anic verses in an altered state and blowing over the patient's body; praying five times a day beseeching Allāh to bestow healing on his patient.

The patient also worked in both worlds. Besides taking medicine, the patient was given sacred prayers to repeat and was taught specific techniques to use as often as possible to help with recovery.

Reflection

Keep your hands busy with your duties in this world
and your heart busy with God.[112]
(Sheikh Muzaffer)

What is the most wondrous sign of the mystic?
That he eats with you, drinks with you, jests with you,
buys from you, sells to you, while his heart is in the Holy Kingdom. This is the most wondrous sign.[113]
(Abū Yazīd Bisṭāmī)

Practices

Contemplate on the following imagery by Rūmī:

❖ You are a traveler charging along your path on a beautiful, strong

[112] Fadiman and Frager, *Essential Sufism*, p. 35.

[113] Sara Sviri, *The Taste of Hidden Things* (Inverness, CA: The Golden Sufi Center, 1997), p. 183.

horse. You traverse many miles; you are happy with your progress. Now you come to the ocean. This horse that sped on land as though it had wings cannot cross the ocean. You now need a different kind of transport to carry you across—a wooden horse. "The wooden horse is this mystical silence: this silence instructs the seafarers."[114] With the active earth-bound horse, you work in the visible world; with the silent seafaring horse, you work in the invisible world. You need both to complete the journey.

[114] Mathnawi VI:4649-4653, C. and K. Helminski, *Jewels of Remembrance*, p. 193.

Second Pillar: Prayer

37

Ṣalāt and *Dhikr*

Celebrate the praises of God morning and evening
[*Sūrah Al-Aḥzāb* 33:42]

THE MULLAH, imprisoned for life, was delighted to hear that his Shaykh or teacher had received permission to visit him. Surely, his beloved teacher would smuggle in a key or weapon to help him get out of jail. The teacher arrived, handed the Mullah a prayer rug and asked him to pray regularly. The Mullah was deeply disappointed. He was expecting something more practical and immediate, something to help him escape. He decided to pray anyhow, prostrating on the prayer rug, as Muslims do five times a day. Over time, the Mullah began to notice a special design in the prayer rug. Upon closer examination, the Mullah realized it was the design of an escape route from the prison!

Muslims have unflinching faith in the grace and power of prayer (called *ṣalāt* in Arabic). To a Muslim, the life of a true believer is a series of unending prostrations. And this magnificent earth, as it revolves through different time zones, becomes a huge prayer rug where one "celebrates the praises of God morning and evening."

Among the countless blessings of prayer, three stand out: taming the ego, purifying the heart, and acquiring a nearness to God.

Through prayer the ego trance that binds us dissolves. The worshiper is graced by an inward disposition to acquire God's attributes and turn away from "transgressions of passions" and "shameful and unjust deeds" [*Sūrah Al-ʿAnkabūt* 29:45]. The center of one's being, one realizes, is not in the ego but in something higher, more essential. Muslims are fond of saying, "One prostration of prayer to God frees you from a thousand prostrations to your ego."

Prayer purifies. The Prophet Muḥammad ﷺ said that prayer was like a flowing river that passes at one's doorstep: "If one of you has a river at his door in which he washes himself five times a day, would it leave any dirt on him? This is an example of the five prayers with which Allāh washes off the evils of man."

Prayer deepens intimacy between the one praising and the One Praised. One attains what the Qurʾān calls *qurb*, a joy of nearness to the Beloved. It is this nearness that made the Prophet ﷺ say, "The freshness of my eyes is given to me in prayer."

Body Prayer and Rituals

The Prophet Muḥammad ﷺ received the inspiration for the ritual prayers in the beatific vision he had in his night journey—the dazzling sight of angels all around him in postures of bowing and prostrating, singing praises of God. The practice of prayer, the Prophet realized, is about praising and thanking God and using the gift of the body to express this adoration.

Islamic legend has it that on his way down to earth from the Divine presence, the Prophet Muḥammad ﷺ met Moses عليه السلام and told him that God had asked that his community pray fifty times a day. "Return to your Lord immediately," advised Moses, "Ask for a lesser number. I know the people; they will never comply." Several times Prophet Muḥammad returned to those mysterious abodes and the number was eventually whittled down to five. When Prophet Moses urged him to return to God for a further reduction, Prophet Muḥammad said he felt embarrassed to ask again.

Islamic tradition says that collective prayer has greater merit than individual prayer, twenty-seven times the spiritual value of the latter. Friday noon prayers are specially valued. A *ḥadīth* reveals that when Friday comes, angels are standing at the door of the mosque awaiting the arrival of God's adorers.

The five-times-a-day ritual prayer is preceded by a call to prayer and an ablution process. The call to prayer is proclaimed aloud by a *muezzin* invoking the Majesty of God and enjoining everyone to come to prayer for their betterment. Some wonder why the *muezzin* has to declare so loudly and repeatedly that God is great. Surely, God who hears the "anklets on the feet of insects"[115] knows this. Islamic teachers explain that this loud declaration is not for God but for us humans. Immersed in the hustle and bustle of life, we humans easily forget what is most Real. For our own good we need constant reminders.

The ritual of ablution is necessary because to come into the presence of Splendor, one must be in a state of purification. Outer cleansing is done with an inner prayer for forgiveness, mercy, and guidance. The Prophet Muḥammad ﷺ said, "Ablution upon ablution is illumination upon illumination."

Preserve Prayer, Especially the Middle Prayer

Grandfather took seriously the counsel from the Qur'ān which says: "Preserve prayer, especially the middle prayer" [*Sūrah Al-Baqarah* 2:238], i.e., make the ritual a prayer from the heart. Grandfather prayed with intense devotion and sincerity. There were several distinct elements to his prayers.

The first element was the physical ritual expressing praise and gratitude. Standing erect, eyes lowered, he raised his outstretched palms to his ears, symbolizing with a sweep that for now he was putting the world behind him and was really listening as he communed with God. After glorifying and expressing heartfelt thanks to God, he bowed in humility and then stood up saying, "God hears those who laud Him." These words are an enunciation by God through the mouth of his adorer. This deepens intimacy between adorer and Adored. Following this came the

---

[115] Bly, *The Kabir Book*, p. 2.

words, "O Lord! Yours is the praise!" This was said aloud by grandfather, the congregation, and also the invisible congregation of angels who Muslims believe are always present in places of devotion. When grandfather prostrated and said, "Glory to my Lord, the Greatest of the Great," he was symbolically in a state of annihilation (*fanāʾ*)—in complete surrender to God. When he sat up, his posture symbolized humility and subsistence (*baqāʾ*)—what remains of one after dissolving in God.

Grandfather repeated this body-ritual a second time and ended by sitting again in a state of humility. He ended this one cycle of prayer by turning his head to the right and left saying each time, "Peace and blessings be upon you." This greeting was meant for the two angels continuously accompanying every human being on the right and on the left, and for the host of angels who had gathered on this occasion.

The second element after completing the cycle of body prayers was a practice of *istaughfurullah*, i.e., seeking forgiveness of God. Grandfather focused on his heart and simply repeated that word in his heart. This repentance was for every thought and action that separated him from his Lord. The practice was modeled after the Prophet Muḥammad's ﷺ inclination to continuously ask God for forgiveness. Because he said it so often, the Prophet was called *Sayyid il istaughfurullah*, "Prince of Forgiveness."

Grandfather expounded on the meaning of *istaughfurullah* to his students. He was eager to tell them that repentance arises not from guilt but from an acknowledgement of our own limited awareness. He explained as follows: "I walked through the mango gardens to come to this prayer place. Unknowingly, I trampled on many ants and insects and destroyed many shelters. God knows how much terror, suffering, and panic I caused in that community. Then, in the course of my day, maybe some words I said or something I did caused pain and grief to some people. For this, for my ignorance and lack of awareness, I ask forgiveness—*istaughfurullah*."

By the mercy of God, Paradise has eight doors –
one of them is the door of repentance, child.
All the others are sometimes open, sometimes shut;

but the door of repentance is never closed.
Come seize the opportunity: the door is open;
carry your baggage there at once.[116]
(Rūmī)

The third element was *du'a* or supplication to God. In the Qur'ān, Allāh says, "Pray unto me and I will hear you" [*Sūrah Ghāfir* 40:60]. Grandfather started by asking blessings for all enlightened beings in various realms, then to his ancestors, especially parents. He begged for God's mercy, grace, and healing for family, friends, and fellow beings. He included prayers for the well being of animals and for an abundance of crop harvests. At the end, he beseeched God for help and guidance for himself.

Grandfather loved to pray. To him prayer was an invitation to the Divine Presence, nectar for the soul, a divine feast! Orthodox Muslims in the village asserted that by not praying five times a day one was sure to incur Allāh's wrath and suffer punishment. Grandfather took the mystical view that by not praying one misses out on a celestial banquet, and that loss is the penalty. Once you've tasted the joy and beauty of praying, your being longs to partake of it again and again.

The heart which has seen the sweetheart,
how should it remain bitter?
When a nightingale has seen the rose,
how should he remain silent?"[117]
(Rūmī)

Dhikr

The Qur'ān says, "Remember God, standing, sitting, and reclining" [*Sūrah An-Nisā'* 4:103]. A *ḥadīth* says, "There is for everything a polish

[116] Mathnawī IV:2506-2508, C. and K. Helminski, *Jewels of Remembrance*, p. 76.
[117] Jalālu'ddin Rūmī, Mathnawī VI:2639, *The Mathnawī of Jalālu'ddin Rūmī,* translated by Reynold A. Nicholson (London, UK: Luzac and Company, Ltd., 1930, reprinted 1982), p. 404.

that takes away rust and the polish of the heart is the invocation of Allāh."

Dhikr literally means invocation or remembrance in Arabic. In this practice, Muslims are asked to repeat God's beautiful names or sacred verses from the Qur'ān as often as possible, not only in formal prayers but in all of one's waking hours.

Some, as a regular practice, do *dhikr* collectively. Joined in a circle they recite, chant, and sing sacred verses. Sometimes these sessions last all night. These friends of the Beloved exult about feeling an astonishing presence descending in their midst, and tasting a sweetness that Islamic mystics say existed before honey or bee. This exquisite sweetness evokes a memory of humankind's closeness to Divinity, of our time in those celestial realms before we arrived here. As Rūmī says:

Before there existed in this world a garden, a vine, a grape,
our soul was drunk on eternal wine.[118]

Words fail to describe this experience. One can only quiver in delight, bewilderment, and gratitude.

When grapes turn to wine,
they're wanting this.
When the night sky pours by,
it's really a crowd of beggars,
and they all want some of this![119]
(Rūmī)

The Qur'ān says, "Truly in the remembrance of God do hearts find peace" [*Sūrah Ar-Ra'd* 13:28].

Reflections

❖ The Sufi Master 'Abdul Qādir Jīlānī relates an incident when he

[118] Harvey, *The Way of Passion*, p. 207.
[119] Mathnawī I:1811, Barks and Moyne, *The Essential Rūmī*, p. 262.

almost missed the early morning prayer but for a cat that nudged him into wakefulness. Gratefully, he finished his prayers in time and then observed, because of his awareness, that the cat was a devil in disguise. Amazed, he asked the cat why he woke him to pray to God. The cat replied, "Because you've discovered me, I might as well tell you. I knew that if you missed your obligatory prayer, you would offer one hundred prayers in compensation, so I woke you up so that you would get only the benefits of the one."[120]

❖ God is Infinite Mercy. It is said that He ignores many of our petitions in prayers because unknown to us, they are filled with loss and destruction.

Forget your life. Say "God is Great!" Get up.
You think you know what time it is. It's time to pray.[121]
(Rūmī)

[120] Fadiman and Frager, *Essential Sufism*, pp. 237-238.
[121] Furuzanfar 2933, translated by C. Barks, *The Rūmī Collection*, p. 132.

THIRD PILLAR: ALMSGIVING

38

Zakāt and *Ṣadaqāt*

Give freely of what you love.
[*Sūrah Āl ʿImrān* 3:92]

SHAMSI TABRIZ, beloved friend and teacher of Rūmī, declared that worship of God is really about honoring and serving ones' fellow beings. Observe, he said, the five-time-a-day worship of Muslims all around the world, prostrating in prayer to the Kaʿbah in Mecca. Joyously, he exclaimed, "The Kaʿbah is in the middle of the world. All faces turn toward it. Take it away. See! Each is bowing to the soul of each."

The Qurʾān enjoins every Muslim to express love for God by serving the destitute and the marginalized in one's community. "Give freely of what you love," counsels the Qurʾān. To the members of his community, the Prophet ﷺ said, "Those who look after widows, orphans, and the destitute are equal to the ones striving in the way of Allāh and, in my eyes, the same as those who worship all night and fast all day."

Almsgiving which is evoked in eighty verses in the Qurʾān has two forms: *zakāt* and *ṣadaqāt*. *Zakāt* literally means "cleansing" and is about purification. Muslims are asked to donate at least 2½% annually of their net worth to those in need. This is ordained by God, says the Qurʾān, and goes on to explain that this giving purifies oneself and one's property.

Ṣadaqāt, which means donation, has to be derived from legitimate funds, honestly gained, and given discreetly. The Qur'an says: "Never shall you attain to true piety unless you spend on others out of what you cherish yourselves; and whatever you spend—verily, God has full knowledge thereof" [*Sūrah Āl ʿImrān* 3:92]. The Islamic Holy Book further elaborates: *It is noble if you make your charity public but far superior is the charity that helps the needy in secret; it will atone for some of your sins* [*Sūrah Al-Baqarah* 2:271].

Unique Service

Whenever grandfather talked about almsgiving, he always ended by saying that each of us has a unique service to offer. Every circumstance, event, and relationship in our life is a preparation for that service. That unique giving of ourselves is our real name and no one knows our real name until the day we die.

Rūmī explains it with a metaphor. A fruit on a tree appears in the end but is really there in the beginning.[122] The fruit is the cause and reason for the sprouting branches, leaves, flowers, and finally the fruit. The fruit of service is one of the reasons for our existence.

Grandfather advised that there is no need to ponder or calculate the grandness of our sacred mission. He told the following story. The Mullah was resting under a large mulberry tree thinking that it would be a nice idea to be of service. "In what ways can I help the world?" he thought to himself. In that moment, an opportunity presented itself, or so it seemed. "Excuse me Allāh," said the Mullah, "It just dawned on me that something is out of balance in Your grand design. This huge mulberry tree bears the tiniest of berries while the weak, flimsy creeper out there grows huge melons. A little symmetry is in order here. Allāh, you understand that I am not criticizing, only trying to be of help." The Mullah felt good about his contribution. In that instant a tiny berry from the high branches fell and landed on the Mullah's head. The Mullah was graced by a deeper insight. "I see! I see! What if the berry had been a melon! Indeed! Let me think of some other way I can be of help."

Our unique mission in life unfolds with beauty and fluidity when we serve in the here and now, in the hundred-and-one opportunities that

---

[122] K. Helminski, *The Rūmī Collection,* p. 14.

come our way each day. In becoming a servant of service at every moment, our sacred mission unfolds, and we become a master of life.

Come dwell at My door and be homeless:
don't pretend to be a candle, be a moth,
so you may taste the savor of Life
and contemplate the sovereignty hidden in servitude.[123]
(Rūmī).

Rūmī says the finest human beings are those who constantly help others.[124] When you become a true servant of service, the Light graces you. You radiate! You become a divine lamp. You do not worry whether you are placed high or low.[125] Already you have been honored by the Light, by God's love for you. What you care about is to shine light to serve others. You want to be of service, joyously and selflessly. You fulfill your unique mission without calculation or self-consciousness.

Reflection

Grandfather repeated often the insight by the Prophet Muḥammad ﷺ that the noblest of service, the holiest of giving, was the service of motherhood. "Paradise lies at the feet of mothers," declared the Prophet. "No matter what you do for your mother you cannot repay as much as one night's due," insisted the Prophet. A persistent questioner asked of the Prophet if he would not be repaying his mother's bounty if he carried his infirm mother on his back for years, fed her, and cared for her in every possible way.

"There would still be this difference," explained the Prophet. "Your mother served you yearning for you to live; you served her waiting for her to die."

---

[123] Mathnawī V:413-414, C. and K. Helminski, *Jewels of Remembrance*, p. 90.
[124] Harvey, *Light Upon Light*, p. 233.
[125] "No Above or Below," translated by A. Harvey, *The Rūmī Collection*, p. 184.

I slept and dreamt that life was joy.
I awoke and found that life was service
I served and lo! Service was joy.
(Tagore)[126]

[126] Quoted by former United Nations Under Secretary General Dr. Robert Muller in the introduction to *A Contribution to the Year 3000* (Santa Barbara, CA: Media 21, http://www.robertmuller.org, 2001).

FOURTH PILLAR: FASTING

39

Ramaḍān

Cultivate in yourself the attributes of God

THE CELEBRATED Night of Power, when the Qur'ān was revealed to the Prophet Muḥammad ﷺ, occurred in the month of Ramaḍān, the ninth month of the Islamic year. To offer gratitude to God for the gift of the Qur'ān, the entire month is designated as a period of self-purification. Muslins abstain from food, drink, and sex, from first light to sunset. During the entire month, Muslims offer special prayers and make fresh commitments to build "self-restraint" [*Sūrah Al-Baqarah* 2:183] and create what a *ḥadīth* calls "a safeguard against moral and spiritual ills." This external fasting is meant to help us with our internal fast.

In vivid metaphorical imagery, a *ḥadīth* tells us that in this sacred month, "The gates of paradise are open, the gates of hell are closed, and the devils are in chains." Use this time wisely, counsels the Prophet ﷺ, to "cultivate in yourself the attributes of God."

Rūmī extols the beauty of fasting. "There is a hidden sweetness in the stomach's emptiness,"[127] he says; "When the body empties and stays empty, God fills it with musk and mother-of-pearl."[128] In another image, Rūmī says that we are lutes, no more, no less, and if the soundbox is

[127] Ode 1739, Moyne and Barks, *Open Secret*, p. 42.
[128] Mathnawi V:148, Barks and Moyne, *The Essential Rūmī*, p. 69.

stuffed full of anything, there is no music.[129]

Ramaḍān is a time to exercise special vigilance over ourselves. May we grow in compassion and forgiveness and become aware of our dependency on God! In a *ḥadīth qudsī,* Allāh says, "Fasting is for Me and I shall grant reward for it Myself."

On the twenty-seventh night of Ramaḍān, the Night of Power, Muslims pay special attention to their prayers. The Qur'ān says that the Night of Power is better than a thousand months and on that night "the angels and the Spirit come down by Allāh's permission" [*Sūrah Al-Qadr* 97:3-4].

According to the Prophet Muḥammad ﷺ, the two joys of fasting—*ifṭār* (breaking the fast at sunset) and *ʿĪd* (the holiday following the sighting of the new moon, signaling the end of Ramaḍān)—have symbolic meaning. The former gives us a taste of paradise in the hereafter and the latter a foretaste of the breathless joy and delight felt in glimpsing God's face on the Day of Judgment.

Grandfather was fond of telling his students that Ramaḍān is the time to redouble efforts to develop in oneself the qualities of graciousness and generosity so that one draws closer to Allāh. He quoted the *ḥadīth*: "The character of the *Walī* (friend of God) is based on nothing but generosity and graciousness."

---

[129] Ode 1739, Moyne and Barks, *Open Secret,* p. 42.

FIFTH PILLAR: PILGRIMAGE

40

Ḥajj

Fulfill the pilgrimage to Mecca for the love of your Lord
[*Sūrah Al-Baqarah* 2:196]

THE QURʾĀN asks every Muslim who is able-bodied and financially able to perform the pilgrimage once in a lifetime by going to the holy city of Mecca and participating in the rituals of *Ḥajj*, all for the love of God. The word means "to set out with a definite purpose."

Muslims are eager to fulfill their sacred duty of pilgrimage, a six-day ritual in the twelfth month of the Islamic calendar. Since this is not possible for everyone, many in villages and towns such as in grandfather's village of Mahdipur, "club together" and elect someone to go on their behalf. They delight in donating money to the one elected, requesting that the person pray for them in the holy places in and around Mecca.

The pilgrim, upon arriving in Mecca, exclaims, "Here I am, O Lord, here I am at Your command." The servant of God joins the global community of Muslims to perform certain rites, the main ones being as follows:

- ❖ Going around the holy Kaᶜbah seven times
- ❖ Visiting the plain of Arafat and praying for forgiveness
- ❖ Going to Minā and casting pebbles at a pillar which marks the place where the devil tempted Abraham عليه السلام and his family
- ❖ Sacrificing an animal and distributing the meat to the poor
- ❖ Completing the farewell circumambulation of the Kaᶜbah

By circling around the Kaʿbah the pilgrim participates with invisible celestial beings in worship of God. In this circumambulation, the human aspires to ascend in closeness to God.

The Qurʾān explains the sacredness of the plain of ʿArafāt. In this place Adam عليه السلام and Eve were reunited on earth. This is also the place where the primordial covenant between God and "as-yet-unborn humanity" was consecrated. Thus, ʿArafāt is a "power spot," a locus of intensified God-consciousness. Here, pilgrims fervently pray for forgiveness and mercy for themselves and others.

In historical Minā, Satan tempted Abraham عليه السلام, Ishmael عليه السلام, and Hagar to disobey God. They successfully withstood the temptations and emerged victorious. The pilgrims in Minā, by casting pebbles at a stone pillar, express their resolve to resist the wiles of Satan in their life.

The sacrifice of an animal represents the sacrifice of one's ego at the altar of God, surrendering to God what is precious to one's own self.

The pilgrimage ends with a farewell circling around the Kaʿbah meant to remind the pilgrim that one's real homeland is in those celestial realms.

Circle of Love

Grandfather dwelled on the fact that a primary joy of *Ḥajj* lay in the ritual of participating in global community for the sake of God. During *Ḥajj,* men and women all wear the same white clothing signifying purity and the truth that in the field of spirit there is no distinction or division. Everyone is joined together for the love of God. *Ḥajj* as a fifth pillar was instituted in 632 A.D. during the Prophet's ﷺ farewell pilgrimage and final sermon, where he extolled the need for community.

Spiritual teachers ask us to reflect deeply on the following question: do we enjoy true community in our personal lives? To interact intimately in a community is not just a good idea; it is a necessity, vital and critical to our development and growth.

Rūmī's prayer for us is that we come out of the circle of time and enter the circle of love. The Master says, "You may be happy enough going alone, but with others you travel in greater security and happiness."[130] In example after example, the Master encourages us to create community.

Every prophet sought out companions.
A wall standing alone is useless
but put three or four walls together,
and they'll support a roof and keep
the grain dry and safe.

When ink joins with a pen, then the blank paper
can say something. Rushes and reeds must be woven
to be useful as a mat. If they weren't interlaced,
the wind would blow them away.
Like that, God paired up
creatures, and gave them friendship.[131]
(Rūmī)

Grandfather took seriously the idea of forming a circle of love in one's life. He asked that we make conscious efforts in this sacred endeavor. Ask yourself, "Who is there in my life who can pass through these three gateways: love, trust, and truth? That is, from this person I receive unconditional love and nurturance in response to love from me; I trust this person and in this person's presence I can be vulnerable and not be judged; and finally, this person loves the truth." Members of the circle can come from the pool of family members and friends.

Notice that the gateways are selective. They allow only a few to pass through. This underlines the sacredness and preciousness of the circle of love in your life. In your association with everyone, always be compassionate, but when it comes to your circle of love, exercise discernment. Have a sense of awareness and patience about this. Especially, be thirsty for the circle.

---

[130] Mathnawi VI:512-518, translated by K. & C. Helminski, *The Rūmī Collection*, p. 9.
[131] Mathnawī VI:518-523, Barks and Moyne, *The Essential Rūmī*, p. 247.

Inner Circle of Love

Several times a week, grandfather gathered with senior disciples and entered into a meditation to bond with an inner circle of love. Through this intimate bonding with an inner community, everyone experienced love, healing, and empowerment.

What is remarkable, grandfather explained, is that while the outer circle of love, which we so desperately need in our lives, might take time to build, we have the power to manifest instantly an inner community. We can experience love and support from this inner circle of love right now.

Grandfather guided his students through a special meditation that focused on the inner circle. In your inner landscape, visit your "sanctuary": a place of safety, beauty, peace, love, healing, and magic. Create such a place. This could be indoors or outdoors.

Once you are there, summon your inner circle of love—anyone that your heart and mind desires—making sure, however, that whoever you bring in passes through the three gateways of love, trust, and truth. Know that in the sanctuary you have the power to bring in whomever you want: persons living or dead, historical beings, spiritual masters, angels, guardian spirits, etc. Your choices are vast.

Then, in your sanctuary, simply be present with the sacred community of your inner circle of love. Bond emotionally with the members and bask in the love they hold for you. It is in their nature to love you. Allow them to nourish and cherish you. Feel them coming close to you if you like; feel them touching and holding you in their embrace. Open up to their love. Remember, it is your birthright to receive unconditional love. Give yourself permission to receive. Your inner circle of love feels ecstatic joy in bestowing upon you love and healing.

As you deepen your relationship with your inner circle, incredible things begin to happen. Your outer circle of love gradually manifests and your intimacy with the outer circle grows sweeter.

Because of his personal experiences, grandfather was enthusiastic in sharing the remarkable fact that you have the power to summon the inner circle of love to help you in your everyday life. Especially when, in your time of need, you connect with truth, love, sincerity, and compassion (from divine attributes in you), the circle arrives instantly! The inner circle of love responds instantaneously to the call and need of the soul.

It is blissful to be blessed with a circle of love, both outer and inner. Mawlana Rūmī says there is a subtle fragrance that comes to you when you are in the presence of His friends: "Sweet is the oneness of the Friend with His friends."[132]

Reflections

"When my slave remembers Me quietly in isolation,
I, too, remember him quietly in My own Being.
But when he remembers Me in a group,
then I remember him better in a group."
(*Ḥadīth* of the Prophet Muḥammad ﷺ)

O heart, sit with someone
who knows the heart;
Go under the tree
which has fresh blossoms.[133]
(Rūmī)

The hearty unripe grapes, capable of ripening,
at last become one in heart
by the breath of the masters of heart.
They grow rapidly to grapehood,
shedding duality and hatred and strife.
Then in maturity, they rend their skins,
till they become one:
unity is the proper attribute

[132] Mathnawi I:682, C. and K. Helminski, *Rūmī Daylight*, p. 28.
[133] Translated by C. Barks; Fadiman and Frager (editors), *Essential Sufism*, p. 102.

for one who is one with others.[134]

(Rūmī)

Practices

As you seek to create an outer circle of love, deepen three qualities in yourself that you seek in others: love, trust, and truth. Ask yourself:

- Am I loving and gentle with myself?
- Do I trust myself—do I really listen to my inner voice?
- Do I honor my heart and act on what I believe in?

Take deliberate steps to create community in your life:

- Connect with a family member you like.
- Get to know your neighbor. Take the initiative.
- Do some volunteer work in the community, working with children, women, the homeless, animal shelters, etc.

Make it a meditative practice to visit from time to time your magical sanctuary and summon your inner circle of love. Give yourself permission to simply be present with the inner circle. Bask in the love they hold for you.

[134] Mathnawī II:3723-3725, C. and K. Helminski, *Rūmī Daylight,* p. 203.

WISDOM FROM PARENTS:

41
Flexibility

Blessed are the Flexible

I HAVE TREASURED an insight that was said repeatedly by my parents and their friends: "Blessed are the flexible, for they will never be bent out of shape!" This was said with light-hearted graciousness to underscore the need for temperance and reasonableness in following the prescriptions of the Qur'ān. The spirit of the Holy Book and examples of the Prophet Muḥammad's ﷺ life emphasize balance and moderation in one's life.

The Qur'ān says, "We have appointed you a moderate nation" [*Sūrah Al-Baqarah* 2:143]. Another verse remarks, "Do not deprive yourselves of the good things of life which God has made lawful to you"; simply do not "transgress the bounds of what is right" [*Sūrah Al-Mā'idah* 5:87-88]. "Beautify yourselves for every act of worship, and eat and drink, but do not waste" [*Sūrah Al-Aʿrāf* 7:31]. A *ḥadīth* advises that you may "eat what you want and dress as you desire as long as extravagance and pride do not mislead you."

The Prophet Muḥammad ﷺ consistently advised moderation. He despaired of well-meaning people in his community who tended to be severe and rigid in their practices. To them he said, "This religion is simple. Don't make it a burden or you shall be overcome."

One of the Prophet's ﷺ companions, ʿUthmān رضي الله عنه, made it his daily practice to fast in the daytime and keep vigil late into the night. The Prophet gently admonished him, "Verily, your eyes have rights over you, and your body has its rights, and your family have their rights."

In ritualistic practices a Muslim is expected to pray, participate in almsgiving, fast, and perform the *Ḥajj.* But the teachings of the Qurʾān, the Prophet Muḥammad ﷺ, saints and mystics, all ask us to concentrate primarily on the sincerity and purity of our intentions. Give your primary attention to essence, not mere appearances; keep practices simple and be balanced in your approach.

The Prophet ﷺ was once approached by a sincere person who said, "Beloved Muḥammad, the legislation of the faith has become too complicated for me; tell me then of one thing to which I can apply myself." The Prophet replied, "Let your tongue be forever moistened with the mention of God Most High."

To another person who was concerned that the urgent but time-consuming work of creating reconciliation between two parties was detracting from his ritual practices, the Prophet ﷺ said, "Renewing peace between two aggrieved parties surpasses ritual prayer, fasting, and almsgiving."

As for the practice of fasting, the Qurʾān is flexible. If you are unable to fast, "it is incumbent on those who can afford it to make sacrifice by feeding a needy person. And whoever does more good than he is bound to do does good unto himself thereby; for to fast is to do good unto yourselves—if you but knew it." [*Sūrah Al-Baqarah* 2:184].

Regarding *Ḥajj,* Islamic saints delight in telling the story of Bisṭāmī, the ninth-century *walī,* who solemnly proceeded on his journey to Mecca intent on fulfilling his sacred duty of pilgrimage. He was particularly eager to perform the ritual of going around the holy Kaʿbah. En route, he met a desperate man who pleaded with Bisṭāmī to give him all his money. The poor man had a family of seven to support. In spite of endless toil and sacrifices, the man was heavily in debt and the family close to starvation. Bisṭāmī gave the man his money. He circled around the man seven times and returned home, joyous that he had completed his sacred pilgrimage.[135]

---

[135] By Attar, *Muslim Saints and Mystics,* translated by A. J. Arberry (London, England: Arkana Penguin Books, 1966), p. 114.

Laughter

The beloved saints in Islām say that many of us are far too severe with ourselves and take life much too seriously. We need discipline and focus but also flexibility, spaciousness, and lots of laughter. A hidden smile from within knows that what is mortal and transient is also grounded in eternity. Truly all is well.

The Persian mystic Ḥāfiẓ points out that the Beloved's nature is pure joy. The closer we come to Him, the more we are able to hear and feel God's laughter. If we don't laugh, it's because we are not yet blessed with higher awareness.

"Isn't it strange?" remarks Rūmī, "that we are being dragged out of our fiery furnaces and smoky hell into paradise and the fragrance of the eternal rose garden, and all we are doing is howling and lamenting."[136] Here we are afraid to go into non-existence, while non-existence is trembling in fear that it might be given human shape![137]

The fourteenth-century Ḥāfiẓ asks, "What is this precious love and laughter budding in our hearts?" Listen to his answer: "It is the glorious sound of a soul waking up!"[138]

---

[136] Discourse 26, paraphrased, Thackston, *Signs of the Unseen*, pp. 121-122.

[137] Mathnawi I:3684, translated by K. and C. Helminski, *The Rumi Collection*, p. 66.

[138] Ḥāfiẓ, *I Heard God Laughing,* versions by Daniel Ladinsky (Walnut Creek, CA: Sufism Reoriented, 1996), p. 125.

42

Journey Home

Verily unto God we are returning
[*Sūrah Al-Baqarah* 2:156]

MULLAH NAṢRUDDĪN was with a party of tourists in the British Museum in London. When the guide pointed to a museum piece and said it was five thousand years old, the Mullah stepped forward with a correction: "Five thousand and four years old." The guide was not amused. The guide went on to another piece and when asked about its antiquity, he answered that it was about two thousand years old. Again, the turbaned and bearded visitor from the east corrected the guide: "No, it's two thousand and four years old." By now, the guide was annoyed: "Sir, I know you come from the mysterious East, but you cannot possibly know the exact dates. What makes you so precise?"

"Simple," replied the Mullah, "I was here four years ago and at that time you mentioned those dates."

One of the many insights from this story is this: It's later than you think. If we are not mindful of time, when the summons comes to cross over to the other side, we are not ready. We find that we had become enmeshed in trivialities. We put off what we really wanted and needed to do and say. We were lulled into forgetting that our stay is temporary. We became overly engrossed in our material conditions here; that became an end in itself and a pointless distraction. One modern teacher asks, "Would you fastidiously decorate and redecorate your hotel room?" We forget we are visitors.

Childhood, youth and maturity,
and now old age.

Every guest agrees to stay
three days, no more.

Master, you told me to
remind you. Time to go.[139]
(Rūmī)

With gentleness grandfather reminded his students that our stay on earth is like the "flicker of a candle placed against eternity." Verily to God we belong and to God we are returning. When we pass on to the other side, our work continues to evolve and unfold in those mysterious, divine realms. May we use our time wisely so that our journey on the other side is easier and fruitful!

Travelers, it is late.
Life's sun is going to set.
During these brief days that you have strength,
be quick and spare no effort of your wings.[140]
(Rūmī)

Death as Spiritual Practice

The Prophet Muḥammad ﷺ meditated often on his own death. The practice expanded his understanding of the mystery of life and deepened his experience of compassion. He once said, "The only preacher you ever need is your death." In the process of reaching important decisions, consult with your death. This exercise very quickly rearranges priorities and values.

Another spiritual practice of the Prophet ﷺ was to visit the dead in graveyards and spend time there in prayer. Often he did this in the middle

---

[139] Barks, *Birdsong*, p. 48.
[140] Mathnawī II:1265-1266, C. and K. Helminski, *Rūmī Daylight*, p. 133.

of the night. In one of his last acts before his transition to the other side, the Prophet prayed all night in a graveyard begging mercy from his Lord for the departed souls. This practice, the Prophet said, builds in us qualities of humility, gentleness, and fearlessness.

A Lovesick Nightingale

The All-Merciful One that brought us here and so quickly carries us away, takes care of all Its loved ones with exquisite tenderness, compassion, love, and honor. Your soul knows this. That is why just before passing on, a celestial light shines in you; for an instant your being glows with joy.

Rūmī says that you have no idea of the joy your soul feels in going home.

At last you have departed and gone to the Unseen.
What marvelous route did you take from this world?
Beating your wings and feathers,
you broke free from this cage.
Rising up to the sky
you attained the world of the soul . . .
As a lovesick nightingale, you flew among the owls.
Then came the scent of the rose garden
and you flew off to meet the Rose.[141]

(Rūmī)

My brother and I glimpsed this briefly at our mother's deathbed. Hospitalized for an unexpected illness, she fought to live. A few moments before her soul passed on, the struggles melted. Time stood still. Her face shone with indescribable serenity. Then her spirit was gone. Instinctively our soul felt the exuberant joy of Mother's soul returning home. A sharp grief met with a strange celebration inside of us.

[141] Star, *Rūmī - In the Arms of the Beloved*, p. 184.

A few days later, our heart-broken father was rushed to the hospital in an unconscious state. At his side, my sister, a medical doctor, saw a sight that is seared in her memory. For an instant, father's eyes popped incredibly wide open holding a gaze that looked beyond in sweet astonishment and bewilderment. What were the celestial wonders that the eyes of his soul were feasting on? He closed his eyes, took his last breath, and dissolved in exquisite surrender.

Oh serene soul!
Return to your Lord
Pleased and pleasing in His sight.
Join my righteous servants
And enter my paradise.
[*Sūrah Al-Fajr* 89:27-30]

Reflections

Do the work that will please your Sustainer.[142]
(Among the last words of the Prophet Muḥammad ﷺ)

Our death is a tax the soul has to pay
for having a name and form.
(Hazrat Inayat Khan)

When we are dead,
seek not our tomb in the earth,
but find it in the hearts of men.
(Rūmī's epitaph on his grave)

When you were born,
everyone was smiling but you were crying.
Live such a life, that, when you depart,

[142] Based on *Islamic Spirituality,* edited by Seyyed Hossein Nasr (New York, NY: The Crossroad Publishing Company, 1987), p. 91.

everyone is weeping but you are smiling.
(*Ḥadīth* of the Prophet Muḥammad ﷺ)

Practices

Grandfather encouraged family and friends to do the following exercise:

- ❖ At the end of the day, review highlights of your actions and reactions. Then ask yourself how these would change if you knew you were to die soon. Using that awareness, in your meditative state, participate in your revised activities and speech, engaging as fully as possible all your sense faculties.

With continuous practice, profound shifts take place. It is as if you are "A stone which has become a ruby filled with the qualities of the sun. No stoniness remains in it."[143]

[143] Mathnawī V:2025-2026, translated by K. Helminski, *The Rūmī Collection,* p. 104.

Biographical Notes

Abū Saʿīd ibn Abīʾl-Khayr (d.1049 CE)

Abū Saʿīd ibn Abīʾl-Khayr was an illustrious master poet and teacher who called himself "a nobody, son of nobody." After a period, lasting until he was 40, of rigorous ascetism and emulating the Prophet ﷺ to the most-minute degree, service of the poor became his spiritual practice. "He begged for the poor, swept mosques, cleaned washing-places, and so on. This 'service of the poor,' conceived principally for self-abasement at first, came ever more to the fore in the course of his life."[144] He once said, "The shortest way to God is to bring comfort to the soul of your neighbor."

Akbar (d. 1605 CE)

A powerful Mughal emperor of India, this illiterate king achieved remarkable distinction as a soldier, administrator, and spiritual aspirant. A devout Muslim, he convened scholars and religious teachers of various faiths from all over the world to study and reflect on the divine unity in all religions. He advocated "universal tolerance" based on his perception of the good in all religions.

ʿAlī ibn Abī Ṭālib (d. 661 CE)

As cousin and son-in-law, ʿAlī ibn Abī Ṭālib ﵁ enjoyed a special relationship with the Prophet ﷺ. He was one of the very first to declare *shahādah.* All his actions were dominated by his dedication to the Prophet and the Qurʾān. He was the fourth Caliph of the Sunnī and the first Imām of the Shīʿī. Besides being courageous on the battlefield, he treated

---

[144] Extract by H. Ritter from *The Encyclopaedia of Islam CD-ROM Edition v.1.0* (Leiden, The Netherlands: Koninklijke Brill N.V, 1999).

his enemies with chivalry and generosity. His celebrated sayings and sermons are embodied in a book called *Nahj al-Balāghah* (The Way of Eloquence). ʿAlī's tomb in Najaf, Iraq, is a pilgrimage site.

Bāyazīd (Abū Yazīd) Bisṭāmī (d. 874 CE)

Bisṭāmī is considered a prime example of Islamic saints who, through ego-annihilation, achieve a state of unity of consciousness. "I have vanished. I glided out of my Bāyazīd-hood as a snake glides from a cast skin. And then I looked. And what I saw was this: lover and Beloved and Love are One."[145] "He wrote nothing, but some five hundred of his sayings have been handed down. In part they are extremely daring and imply a state of mind in which the mystic has an experience of himself as of one merged with the deity and turned into God. . . . His passionate aspiration is aimed at absolutely freeing himself through systematic work upon himself ("I was the smith of my own self"), of all obstacles separating him from God, with the object of 'attaining to Him'."[146] He once uttered that he would refuse to exchange the eight Paradises and sovereignty of both worlds "for that single sigh which arises at morning-time from the depth of my soul in remembering my longing for Him."

Bilqīs, the Queen of Sheba (Sabāʾ in the Qurʾān)

The Qurʾān [*Sūrah An-Naml* 27:20-44] describes a transformative incident during a visit by Bilqīs, whose people worshipped the sun, to King Solomon عليه السلام. "She mistook the polished floor of his court for water and raised her skirt to cross it. When she realized her error, and thereby the power of illusion, she accepted the *shahādah*, or testimony of Islam, and surrendered to God. Bilqīs has come to symbolize the nature of woman as infinitude, in complement to man as center and intellect, which Solomon represented."[147]

---

[145] Cyril Glassé, *The Concise Encyclopedia of Islam* (New York, NY: Harper Collins, 1989), p. 76.

[146] H. Ritter, *The Encyclopaedia of Islam CD-ROM Edition v.1.0.*

[147] Glassé, *The Concise Encyclopedia of Islam*, p. 74.

Dārā Shikoh (d. 1659 CE)

Dārā Shikoh was a Muslim prince of Mughal descent in India. He made it his lifelong mission to reconcile Islam and Hinduism. His book *The Meeting of the Two Seas* (its title based on *Sūrah Al-Kahf* 18:60) was a comparative study of the technical terms in Vedanta and mystical Islam. He translated the *Upanishads* into Persian. A Latin version of this translation introduced the *Upanishads* to the West in the late 18th century. "Dārā occupies a preeminent place among those who stood for the concept of universal toleration and who desired that the state should be based on the support of both Muslims and Hindūs, and remain essentially above religion."[148]

Ḥāfiẓ (d. 1391 CE)

A beloved sage and poet of Persia, Ḥāfiẓ is famous for his *Dīwān*, a collection of poetry that is considered oracular. He composed some of the world's most sublime poetry and is considered the master of the *ghazal* form. A translation of his *Dīwān* was known to Goethe at the time when he wrote his *West-ostlicher Diwan*. Ḥāfiẓ is celebrated for the subtlety of his insights, free spirit, and outrageous humor. "Scholars living in an age of non-representational art and literature are perhaps less concerned than most of their forebears. . .to discover positively 'whether Ḥāfiẓ meant what he said,' whether he was a mystic or a libertine, a good Muslim or a skeptic, or all of these by turns. It is now generally claimed (without prejudice) merely that he spoke through the standard themes and terminology of hedonism, the lament for mortality, human and mystical love, and so on; that he was a superb linguistic and literary craftsman, who took these forms so far beyond the work of his predecessors that he practically cut off all succession; and that he revolutionized the *ghazal* and the panegyric both, by making the one the vehicle for the other in place of the *qaṣīda*."[149]

---

[148] S. Chandra, *The Encyclopaedia of Islam CD-ROM Edition v.1.0.*
[149] G.M. Wickens, *The Encyclopaedia of Islam CD-ROM Edition v.1.0.*

Hagar

Islamic stories abound about the overflowing compassion Hagar bore for her son, Ismāᶜīl عليه السلام (Ishmael). When Hagar and Ismāᶜīl were in the wilderness and the "water in the goat skin" given by Abraham عليه السلام was spent, Hagar ran between the two hills of Aṣ-Ṣafā and Al-Marwah several times in desperate search for water. God heard the anguished pleas and cries of Hagar and Ismāᶜīl (Ishmael means "God hears") and miraculously the spring of ZamZam gushed forth from the earth. To "run" between the two hills is a pilgrimage rite for Muslims. As the Northern Arabic people trace their ancestry back through Ismāᶜīl and Hagar, the Prophet Muḥammad ﷺ was descended from them.

Ḥasan al-Baṣrī (d. 728 CE)

Born the son of a freed slave in Medina, Ḥasan al-Baṣrī is one of the great figures of early Islam. He is an important link in the transmission of many *ḥadīth*, having known several of the Prophet's ﷺ companions in Medina. He was famous for his sincerity, religious principles, and ascetic piety, which made a deep impression on his contemporaries. Ḥasan al-Baṣrī said: "The world is a bridge upon which you cross but upon which you should not build" and "Keep polishing your hearts for they quickly grow rusty."

Ibrāhīm ben Adḥam (d. 783 CE)

Of Arab descent and born a prince of Balkh, Ibrāhīm ben Adḥam traveled westward to Syria after giving up his kingdom. His first teacher was a Christian monk named Simeon. Of the path of knowledge, Ibrāhīm ben Adḥam said, "This is the sign of the knower, that his thoughts are mostly engaged in meditation, his words are mostly praise and glorification of God, his deeds are mostly devotion, and his eye is mostly fixed on the subtleties of Divine action and power."[150]

Ismāᶜīl (Ishmael)

Ismāᶜīl عليه السلام was the older son of Abraham عليه السلام by Hagar. While the

[150] Glassé, *The Concise Encyclopedia of Islam*, pp. 177-178.

Qurʾān does not mention by name that Ismāᶜīl was the son to be sacrificed by Abraham, Muslims generally presume this to be so. He is an exemplar for patience, piety, and steadfastness in the face of adversity. It is believed that Abraham visited Hagar and Ismāᶜīl in Mecca after leaving them there at Sarah's insistence. Together Ismāᶜīl and Abraham rebuilt the Kaᶜbah as a temple to the One God, replacing a temple originally built by Adam عليه السلام. In *Sūrah Baqarah* [2:127-129], the Qurʾān says: *And when Abraham and Ishmael were raising the foundations of the Temple, they prayed: "O our Sustainer! Accept Thou this from us: for, verily, Thou alone art all-hearing, all-knowing! O our Sustainer! Make us surrender ourselves unto Thee, and make out of our offspring a community that shall surrender itself unto Thee, and show us our ways of worship, and accept our repentance: for, verily, Thou alone art the Acceptor of Repentance, the Dispenser of Grace! O our Sustainer! Raise up from the midst of our offspring an apostle from among themselves, who shall convey unto them Thy messages, and impart unto them revelation as well as wisdom, and cause them to grow in purity: for, verily, Thou alone art almighty, truly wise!* Ismāᶜīl is considered a prophet (*rasūl*) and the ancestor of the North Arabians. In *Sūrah Maryam* [19:54-55], it says: *And call to mind, through this divine writ, Ishmael. Behold, he was always true to his promise, and was an apostle of God, a prophet, who used to enjoin upon his people prayer and charity; and found favor in his Sustainer's sight.* Ismāᶜīl and Hagar are buried close to the Kaᶜbah.

ᶜAbdul Qādir Jīlānī (d. 1166 CE)

What is known of the life of ᶜAbdul Qādir Jīlānī is mostly legendary and hagiographic. He didn't marry or begin teaching until he was 49. This celebrated teacher, sometimes referred to as the *Quṭb* (spiritual axis) of his age, specialized in what was called "the science of spiritual states." ᶜAbdul Qādir resolved, through his example and teaching, a dichotomy existing in his time between being a pious Muslim or an emotional Sufi. "The fulfillment of works of supererogation [religious practices beyond those required by the Qur'ān] assumes the prior fulfillment of the demands of divine law. Ecstatic practices, though not forbidden, are allowed only with certain restrictions. Ascetism is limited by the duties towards family and society. The perfect sufi lives in his divine Lord, [and] has a knowledge of the mystery of God. . . . Sufism as taught by the Ḥanbalite ʿAbdul Qādir consists in fighting, in a *jihād* greater than the holy war fought with weapons, against self-will; in thus conquering the hidden *shirk*, i.e. the idolatry of self and, in general, of creaturely things; in recognizing in all good and evil the will of God and living, in submission to His will, according to His law."[151] He was the founder of the Qādiriyyah Sufi Order, which was the first *ṭarīqah* (Sufi Order). His most famous writing is *Futūḥ-al-Ghayb* (Revelation of the Unseen).

Joseph (Yūsuf in the Qurʾān)
Joseph عليه السلام was a prophet, an interpreter of dreams, and an exemplar of self-restraint. In the sūrah of Yūsuf [12], the point is made that those whom God protects, no one can destroy. Joseph was the favorite son of his father, Jacob عليه السلام. Due to a plot of his brothers, Joseph was sold into slavery, to a great Egyptian man. The wife of his owner was so overcome with Joseph's beauty that she attempted to seduce him. He did not comply, though he desired her. In spite of the evidence that he had resisted (his shirt was torn in back rather than in front), he was imprisoned. While in prison, he interpreted the dreams of two of Pharaoh's servants. His interpretations were accurate, and when the Pharaoh had disturbing dreams, the servant who had been in prison with Joseph remembered him. The recommendation made by Joseph in his interpretation of the Pharaoh's dream, that grain be saved against threat of famine, has served Muslim governments as a model for social planning. His brothers came to Joseph in the famine to ask for food. The shirt he sent back to his father with them restored Jacob's vision, which he had lost in weeping for Joseph.

---

[151] W. Braune, *The Encyclopaedia of Islam CD-ROM Edition v.1.0.*

Abū'l-Qāsim Muḥammad al-Junayd (d. 910 CE)

Al-Junayd was a well-known teacher in Baghdad, known as the Sultan of the *ʿārifīn* (knowers of God). He said that since all things have their origin in God, they must finally return, after their dispersion, to live again in Him (*jamʿ*); the mystic achieves this in the state of *fanāʾ*. He recommended the integration of mysticism into ordinary life. Rather than be wandering beggars, he suggested Sufis remember Allāh in their daily life, earning a living in the world and being married; he was a merchant and had a shop in Baghdad. Wary of "drunken ecstasy," this famous master wrote, "There is a sobriety that contains all drunkenness, but there is no drunkenness that contains all sobriety."

Kabīr (d. 1518 CE)

Born into a Muslim weaver family in Benares, India, this illiterate saint combined imageries and ideas from the religions of Hinduism and Islam to create simple, ecstatic utterances. His poetry stresses the importance of the teacher and worship using the Name of God. His love of God has touched the hearts of Hindus and Muslims alike for centuries. There is a beautiful story about his death. Both Muslims and Hindus fought over his body. Kabir appeared in spirit and asked them to lift the shroud from the dead body. Instead of a corpse, they discovered a large bouquet of flowers, which they then divided equally.

Khadījah (d. 619 CE)

Khadījah ﵇ was the first wife of Muḥammad ﷺ and the first to profess her belief in God's message as revealed through him. She is revered in Islam as the "protectress" of the Revelation, "guardian angel" of the Prophet, and the first "mother of the faithful." Khadījah bore two sons (who died in infancy) and four daughters, including Fāṭimah ﵇. The Prophet Muḥammad was deeply devoted to her and had no other wives while she was alive. Upon her death, he buried her with his own hands in the al-Malāʾ cemetery in Mecca.

Hazrat Inayat Khan (d. 1927 CE)
A noted Islamic spiritual teacher and musician, Hazrat Inayat Khan taught Islamic mysticism in the United States and Europe from 1910-1927. He aimed to make spirituality relevant to life by bringing the insights gained in mystical experience to bear on our actions, relationships, and aspirations. He said, "Music is nothing less than the picture of our Beloved. . . . In the presence of the Beautiful, man forgets himself."

Moses (Mūsā in the Qurʾān)
A Divine Messenger who brought a new revelation (Judaism and the Mosaic Law), Moses عليه السلام is mentioned in the Qurʾān as often as the Prophet Muḥammad ﷺ. He is considered a precursor of the Prophet. The Qurʾān describes itself as confirming the teachings revealed to Abraham عليه السلام and Moses in verses such as *Sūrah Al-Aʿlā* 87:18-19: *This indeed was in the first revelations, the revelations of Abraham and Moses.* While Moses appears to be limited by the exoteric law or *sharīʿah* in his encounters with al-Khiḍr عليه السلام [*Sūrah Al-Kahf* 18:60-83], Moses had found him as a result of his search for greater knowledge of God. God gives Moses many signs to convince Pharaoh to let the people of Israel go. One of the signs is that Moses' hand becomes shining white, without blemish, when he draws it from his bosom [*Sūrah Al-Aʿrāf* 7:108, *Sūrah Ṭā Hā* 20:22, *Sūrah An-Naml* 27:12, *Sūrah Al-Qaṣaṣ* 28:32], signifying that his activity in the world had become sacred.

Rābiʿa al-ʿAdawiyya (d. 801 CE)
Rābiʿa was one of the most beloved saints; she extolled the way of Divine Love and intimacy with God. She is one of those about whom the Qurʾān says, *But those of faith are overflowing in their love for God* [*Sūrah Al-Baqarah* 2:165]. She emphasized loving God for His own sake alone, not out of fear of Hell or hope for Paradise. She once said, "I love God; I have no time left in which to hate the devil." Her mystical sayings and stories of her ascetic life are cherished in the Islamic world. She is reported to have said to a friend, "Will God forget the poor because of

their poverty or remember the rich because of their riches? Since He knows my state, what have I to remind Him of? What He wills, we should also will." Perhaps the most famous of her prayers is one she made at night on her roof: "O Lord, the stars are shining and the eyes of men are closed and kings have shut their doors and every lover is alone with his beloved and here am I alone with You."

Shamsuddīn Tabrīzī (d. 1248 CE)
Shamsuddīn Tabrīzī was the beloved teacher and friend who transformed Jalālu'ddin Rūmī and brought him to taste direct knowledge. Their meeting in 1244 CE is one of the extraordinary episodes of history. Shamsuddīn, "knower of divine secrets," prayed with deep intensity: "Among the intimates of God, is there no one to bear this?" A voice came from the world of Mystery: "Among those who exist, Jalālu'ddin Rūmī is your friend." After a remarkable meeting, Jalālu'ddin and Shamsuddīn spent days, weeks, and months in mysterious communion. The hours spent in secret transmission lead to jealousies and difficulties in the community. Twice Shamsuddīn left Konya. The second time he never returned. It was rumored that he had been murdered, but his body was never found. About their sharing, Rūmī uttered:

Those tender words we said to one another
Are stored in the secret heart of heaven.
One day, like the rain they will fall and spread
And their mystery will grow green over the world.[152]

Abū Bakr ash-Shiblī (d. 945 CE)
Ash-Shiblī was a noted disciple of al-Junayd, a scholar of ḥadīth, and a teacher in Baghdad. While he left no writings, many of his sayings were recorded. He quoted poets of romantic love, applying their descriptions to love of God. He was very demanding of his students and remained influential on those in government up to his death.

[152] Harvey, *The Way of Passion*, p. 2.

Solomon (Sulaymān b. Dā'ūd in the Qur'ān)

The Qur'ān portrays Solomon عليه السلام as a prophet and King who was a paragon of wisdom with vast knowledge of the unseen world. At an early age he showed his skill in administering justice, even surpassing his father David عليه السلام [*Sūrah Al-Anbiyā'* 21:78-79]. He was acquainted with the language of birds and animals; this allowed him to save a colony of ants when his army was on the move [*Sūrah An-Naml* 27:17-19]. He was reported to have powers over the subtle world. There are many miraculous stories associated with him, some of them expressed in passages in the Qur'ān.

Rabindranath Tagore (d. 1941 CE)

This much-adored Indian national figure was a poet, novelist, playwright, songwriter, and music composer. He said "You can't cross the sea merely by staring at the water." Some of his works capture a feeling of joy and delight in the simplest pleasures of everyday living, like watching a baby sleep or children playing at the seashore. He was the first Asian to receive a Nobel Prize in literature, in 1913.

Sahl at-Tustarī (d. 896 CE)

A Sunnī theologian and a founder of the Sālimiyya school, Sahl at-Tustarī was known for his commentaries on the Qur'ān. He focused on constantly turning to God in repentance (*tawbah*), complete trust in God (*tawakkul*), and the centrality of *dhikr*. His method of recollecting God was to constantly repeat internally, "God is my witness" (*Allāhu shāhidī*). "Sahl at-Tustarī explained the famous saying of the Prophet ﷺ (*ḥadīth*): "I am He and He is I, save that I am I, and He is He" (*ana huwa, wa huwa ana, ghayra an ana ana, wa huwa huwa*) as a mystery of union or realization at the center of the Saint's personality, called the *sirr* (the "secret"), or the heart, where existence joins Being. He said: "God is [only] known by the union of contraries attributed to Him."[153]

---

[153] Glassé, *The Concise Encyclopedia of Islam*, p. 342.

Bibliography

Arberry, A.J. *Doctrine of the Sufis.* Cambridge, UK: University Press, 1978.

Arberry, A. J. *Muslim Saints and Mystics*; London, England: Arkana Penguin Books, 1966.

Chittick, Willliam. *The Sufi Path of Love*, Albany, NY: State University of NY Press, 1983.

The Encyclopaedia of Islam CD-ROM Edition v. 1.0 Leiden, The Netherlands: Koninklijke Brill N.V, 1999.

Fadiman, James and Robert Frager, editors. *Essential Sufism.* San Francisco, CA: Harper, 1997.

Glassé, Cyril. *The Concise Encyclopedia of Islam.* New York, NY: Harper Collins, 1989.

Ḥāfiẓ. *I Heard God Laughing.* Versions by Daniel Ladinsky. Walnut Creek, CA: Sufism Reoriented, 1996.

Harvey, Andrew. *Light Upon Light.* Berkeley, CA: North Atlantic Books, 1996.

Harvey, Andrew and Eryk Hanut. *Perfume of the Desert.* Wheaton, IL: The Theosophical Publishing House, 1992.

Harvey, Andrew. *Teachings of Rūmī.* Boston, MA: Shambhala Publications, 1999.

Harvey, Andrew. *The Way of Passion.* Berkeley, CA: Frog Ltd, 1994.

Helminski, Kabir. *The Knowing Heart*, Boston, MA: Shambhala Publications, 1999.

Kabir. *The Kabir Book.* Versions by Robert Bly. Boston, MA: Beacon Press, 1977.

Muller, Robert. *A Contribution to the Year 3000.* Santa Barbara, CA: Media 21, http://www.robertmuller.org, 2001.

Nasr, Seyyed Hossein, editor. *Islamic Spirituality.* New York, NY: The Crossroad Publishing Company, 1987.

Padwick, Constance E. *Muslim Devotions.* Oxford, England: One World Publication, 1996.

Rūmī, Jalālu'ddin. *Birdsong.* Versions by Coleman Barks based on translations by A.J. Arberry. Athens, GA: Maypop, 1993.

Rūmī, Jalālu'ddin. *Breathing Truth.* Translated by Muriel Maufroy. London, England: Sanyar Press, 1997.

Rūmī, Jalālu'ddin. *The Essential Rūmī.* Translated by Coleman Barks with John Moyne. New York, NY: HarperCollins, 1995.

Rūmī, Jalālu'ddin. *Jewels of Remembrance.* Versions by Camille and Kabir Helminski. Putney, VT: Threshold Books, 1996.

Rūmī, Jalālu'ddin. *Love is a Stranger.* Versions by Kabir Helminski. Putney, VT: Threshold Books, 1993.

Rūmī, Jalālu'ddin. *The Mathnawī of Jalālu'ddin Rūmī.* Translated by Reynold A. Nicholson. London, UK: Luzac and Company, Ltd., © 1930, reprinted 1982.

Rūmī, Jalālu'ddin. *Open Secret.* Translated by John Moyne and Coleman Barks. Putney, VT: Threshold Books, 1984.

Rūmī, Jalālu'ddin. *Poems of Rūmī.* Versions by Robert Bly and Coleman Barks. S. San Francisco, CA: Audio Literature, 1989.

Rūmī, Jalālu'ddin. *The Rūmī Collection.* Edited by Kabir Helminski. Boston, MA: Shambhala Publications, 1999.

Rūmī, Jalālu'ddin. *Rūmī Daylight.* Versions by Camille and Kabir Helminski. Boston, MA: Shambhala Publications, 1999.

Rūmī, Jalālu'ddin. *Rūmī – In the Arms of the Beloved.* Translated by Jonathan Star. NYC, NY: Jeremy P. Tarcher/ Putnam, 1997.

Rūmī, Jalālu'ddin. *Say I Am You.* Translated by John Moyne and Coleman Barks. Athens, GA: Maypop, 1994.

Rūmī, Jalālu'ddin. *Signs of the Unseen.* Translated by William Thackston. Putney, VT: Threshold Books, 1994.

Rūmī, Jalālu'ddin. *The Soul of Rūmī.* Versions by Coleman Barks. New York, NY: Harper Collins, 2001.

Rūmī, Jalālu'ddin. *This Longing.* Translated by Coleman Barks and John Moyne. Putney, VT: Threshold Books, 1988.

Rūmī, Jalālu'ddin. *Unseen Rain.* Translated by John Moyne and Coleman Barks. Putney, VT: Threshold Books, 1986.

Shah, Idries. *The Way of the Sufi.* London, England: Penguin Books, 1974.

Sviri, Sara. *The Taste of Hidden Things.* Inverness, CA: The Golden Sufi Center, 1997.

Tagore, Rabindranath. *Fireflies.* New York, NY: Macmillan Publishing Company, 1955.

Vaughan-Lee, Llewellyn, editor. *Travelling the Path of Love.* Inverness, CA: The Golden Sufi Center, 1995.

تم بحمد الله

Finished, with all praise to Allāh.

Printed in the United States
22316LVS00005B/283-297

9 781904 510086